MYTHS AND ECOSOPHY

A STUDY OF MYTHS, LEGENDS AND FOLKLORE FROM THE PERSPECTIVE OF DEEP ECOLOGY

SAKTI SEKHAR DASH

ISBN 979-888530933-2

***

I dedicate this work to God for the inspiration, my parents for their never-ending support, my teachers for their encouragement and my students for their love and appreciation.

***

Contents

About The Author

The author is a Fellow of Social Science Research Council, Open Association of Research, USA. He is currently engaged in the Department of English, Ravenshaw University as a research scholar. His research interests include Classical literature, Modern Poetry and Absurd Drama. His specialization is American literature. An avid scholar of mythology and folklore, he has studied the Indian, Greek, Roman and Norse myths. He is deeply interested in various cultures, extensively exploring the history and the manner in which it has shaped different cultures. His works include, *The Darts of Death, The Divine Verdict, Death's Dream Kingdom, The Grim World of Fairy Tales, Ruins and Recollections* and *Songs of Solitude.*

Foreword

Climate change and ecological destruction have taken their toll on the planet. Many species of flora and fauna are extinct and many more are headed that way. The human community has treated ecology and the natural environment as the 'other', which has triggered the ecological crisis. There is a clear divide between the humans and non-human nature. But calls have been growing for the need to preserve the ecology. The likes of Rachel Carson, Arne Naess, George Sessions, and Bill Devall have been at the forefront of the environmental movement. They have largely concentrated on building a stable and sustainable relationship between the human community and the natural environment. The ecological philosophy put forth by the environmentalists was rooted in respect for the environment. Deep Ecology and Ecosophy are the prominent ecological movements that sought to revive the relationship between the humans and the ecology.

This work examines the myths and cultural beliefs of various communities and seeks to understand the ecological wisdom contained within their practices. Myths, legends, folklore and ritualistic beliefs have been the building blocks of the human civilization, containing the seeds of timeless wisdom. By examining and exploring the myths and cultural beliefs, the human community can come to terms with the relationship between the humans and the ecology.

Sakti Sekhar Dash

Preface

We are living in the age of ecological destruction and climate change. Due to anthropocentric beliefs, humans consider the environment as a reservoir of resources meant for human consumption and use. Deforestation and hunting have led to the extinction of several species of wildlife. Disruptive human activities have led to the destruction of ecology, the land, resources and non-human species. Anthropocene, which represents a new geological epoch in which humanity has become the main driver of rapid changes in the earth system. At the same time, it highlights that a potentially fatal ecological rift has arisen between human beings and the earth, emanating from the conflicts and contradictions of the modern capitalist society. The planet is now dominated by a technologically potent but alienated humanity—alienated from both nature and itself; and hence ultimately destructive of everything around it. At issue is not just the sustainability of human society, but the diversity of life on Earth. It is common today to see this ecological rift simply in terms of climate change, which given the dangers it poses and the intractable problems for capitalism it presents has grabbed all the headlines.

Social science today is crippled not only by its growing failure to confront the historical specificity and thus the hegemonic structures of present-day society, but also by its repeated refusal to engage critically with the reality of the natural world. Thus, the social sciences and the humanities in particular fields such as economics, political science, sociology, cultural anthropology, philosophy, and cultural studies are all characterized to varying degrees by their radical separation from nature—from the concerns that preoccupy natural science, and more particularly from notions of natural history or evolution. The long revolt against positivism and the domination of the social sciences by natural-scientific conceptions has of course been crucial to the development of today's social sciences/humanities. However, the anthropocentrism and culturalism, and the extreme neglect of natural/material conditions, that this has given rise to, has proven increasingly debilitating, especially in the present age of planetary ecological crisis.

The word *nature,* we should interject here, is one of the more complex words in modern language, standing as it does in different contexts for the material world and even the universe; the most fundamental domain of existence; the elemental drives of life; the object of natural science; certain timeless, immutable laws; evolution; the nonhuman and non-social; the non-intellectual and non-spiritual, and so on.

In declaring its independence from nature viewed as the object of natural science social science has all too often reacted to an earlier Newtonian mechanism that saw nature primarily in terms of timeless, immutable laws. Here the resistance is often to nature as "essentialism" in its various forms, whereby human beings/society are reduced to mere biological entities/by-products often in grossly distorted ways as in classical racist and sexist ideologies. From this perspective, nature stands for what is fixed and unchanging, or changing too slowly to be of direct relevance to human society. John Bellamy Foster explains:

> *"It thus became customary in the social sciences to view the realm of humanity/society/culture/ the mind as a realm constructed apart from nature. Such anthropocentric views were reinforced by the so-called conquest of nature associated with modern science and technology, feeding a "Human-Exemptionalist Paradigm," or the notion that human beings were not only exempt from nature's general laws but could transcend them in almost infinite ways, given ingenuity. Nature was taken for granted, as the social world existed outside the bounds and limits of natural influences. It was assumed that whatever social problems arose in relation to nature, scientific-technological fixes could be employed to maintain the existing social order. As a result, the environmental sustainability of human societies was not a problem. (27)"*

The development of ecology and today's earth system including climate science reflects the movement toward complex, historical, materialist, holistic forms of analysis, taking account of contingency—very far removed from the supposed mechanistic laws of Newtonian science. Indeed, the growing planetary ecological crisis has given rise to an understanding of how fast nature can change under certain conditions and of the coevolution of humanity and nature. Peter M. Vitousek, an ecologist, notes that humans are forcing qualitative and historical changes on the world that will eventually alter the structure and function of Earth as a system. Nature consists of dynamic systems with many parts and functions. Among these systems are ecosystems. Humans are part of ecosystems, and participate in the processes that change them through time. History must take account of the importance and complexity of these processes.

The human species evolved within the community of life by competing against, cooperating with, imitating, using, and being used by other species. Thus, our species is an offspring of the interacting forms of life on Earth. This means not only that human bodies achieved their forms through evolution, but that the ecosystems of the Earth provided our ancestors with sustenance, set problems for them, sharpened their wits, and to a large extent showed them the way they must go.20 Humans, to more impressive degree than any other species, have made ecosystems what they are. That is, humans and the rest of the community of life have been engaged in a process of coevolution. That process continues to the present day. History's job includes examining the record of the changing roles the human species has enacted within the biotic community, some of them more successful than others, and some more destructive than others.

The idea of environment as something separate from the human, and offering merely a setting for human history, is misleading. Whatever humans have done to the rest of the community has inevitably affected themselves. The living connections of humans to the communities of which they are part must be integral components of the historical account. Humans operate *within* the principles of ecology, and must continue to do so as long as the species is to survive.

That all human societies, everywhere and throughout history, have existed within and depended upon biotic communities is true of huge cities as well as small farming villages and hunter clans. The connectedness of life is a fact. Humans never existed in isolation from the rest of life, and could not exist alone, because they depend on the complex and intimate associations that make life possible. To a very large extent, ecosystems have influenced the patterns of human events. Consequently, the narratives of history must place human events within the context of local and regional ecosystems, and world history must in addition place them within the ecosphere, the worldwide ecosystem.

Colonialism has played no small part in disrupting the ecologies and nature systems. Involving brutal subjugation, colonialism has resulted in the destruction of societies, economies and cultures. The age of modern colonialism was triggered by the Age of Discovery. Explorers began to look for new sea routes to facilitate trade. The Spirit of Inquiry prompted the explorers to look for civilisations, for exotic races of humans from fabled lands. In 1415, the Portuguese conquered the small coastal town of Ceuta located in North Africa. This laid the foundation stone for imperialism that would last well into late 20th century. Very soon, the Portuguese conquered the islands of Madeira and Cape Verde and established colonies to facilitate trade.

The colonial ventures and imperial ambitions of the Portuguese led the Spanish, Dutch and the British to look for new sea routes and lands to colonise. The year 1492 is a particularly significant one; Christopher Columbus discovered the New World. With his fleet, Columbus hoped to discover the sea route to India. What he managed to accomplish was the discovery of America.

"The lands of the Western Hemisphere, which include North, Central, and South America, were not "new" to the Indians who already lived here" (McNeese 14). The explorers and settlers looking to colonise the continents of Africa and America encountered wilderness and "savage" tribes. This sparked a conflict between the natives and the imperial powers and resulted in bloodbaths that destroyed several indigenous communities and cultures.

Colonial ventures involved a systematic exploitation of the land, resources and native communities. The land was mined for the ores of precious metals and gemstones; forests were cleared to feed the timber industry. Animals and birds were killed indiscriminately to protect the agricultural lands; colonialism also led to the growth of the fur and pelt industry and exotic animals were hunted for their hides and fur. The colonisers never took into account the ramifications of their actions. Traditional communities that had existed for thousands of years in harmony with the land and the ecology were dislocated culturally and geographically by the imperial powers.

The indigenous and native communities had coexisted for centuries with the ecology. Their lives, cultural practices, ritualistic beliefs, religion, myths and folklore had been woven around the human community's ties with the ecology. The traditional wisdom aimed at preserving the human-nature relationship. However, colonialism disrupted the fabric of coexistence. Not only did the European settlers treat non-human nature as the 'other' but also branded the native cultures and their practices as primitive.

The impact of human civilization in the contemporary world appears inescapable. Certainly, it is the case that wild biotic communities are rapidly disappearing, to say nothing of the accelerating rate of extinction of whole species. Directly correlated with these phenomena is the sharp decline in the number and variety of natural ecosystems. The effects of human culture and technology on the planetary biosphere are becoming ubiquitous. Due to the emergence of large-scale industrialization in the past century, the recent rise in the growth rate of human population, and the expansion of economies that stimulate and depend on high levels of consumption, our human presence is now felt throughout the Earth. It is not only where we have taken over land areas to grow our food crops and to build our towns and cities that ecological changes have been brought about; the physical, chemical, and biological concomitants of modern civilization can be found everywhere. Unless these dominant trends of our age are brought under control, we will see the natural environment of our planet turned into a vast artifact. A massive transformation has already begun not only of the entire land surface of the Earth but also of the open oceans and the very atmosphere itself.

Art, religion, and intellectual life also require a healthy environment. Artists cannot paint if the air they breathe is polluted, nor can scientists proceed with experiments. “Be fruitful and multiply” will be a recipe for disaster when the population exceeds the carrying capacity of the planet. But long before that, the air may be damaged beyond repair by the burning of forests to create more cropland to feed ever more human mouths. The sacredness of life that is recognized by all religions, especially in the East, must be expanded to include the lives of non-humans. The model of Noah’s Ark must replace that of conquest, tribalism, and destruction.

Similarly, the values of happiness, of the self (self-interest), and of personal feelings are chimeras without an environment. As John Dewey realized, we are part of an environment at all times, regardless of our technical prowess at altering it to suit us—a habitat, whether natural or artificial. Indeed, the natural-artificial distinction does not apply, since both are environments.1 Technology cannot do away with the needs of survival of a biological species. We are inseparable from our environment. No human values can be achieved without the most universal condition of all, the environmental conditions of human and all other life. To destroy our environment is to destroy ourselves: it is suicidal.

In short, the environment is not a luxury whose value is debatable, but a requirement of all life, and particularly of human life, and thereby of all human values. Since the environment is required by all life it is a universal requirement, and generates duties. Its value is not instrumental, but inherent. More, it is the condition of all values, and thus prior to all other values as their basis. Environmental ethics is the other that constitutes first philosophy. For the biosphere is the framework for all other values. Thus the distinction of human and environmental ethics ought to be superceded. Universality of obligation must include other self-actualizing agents qua universal: other species.

Ecocentrism is more than just an ethic. Ecocentrism also includes the idea that philosophy should center on environmental concerns and issues, not anthropocentric ones. The mainstream in philosophy, following in René Descartes footsteps, is still debating essentially sixteenth century ideas regarding knowledge: representationalism versus non-representationalism, subjectivism versus objectivism, and the like. Ecocentrism sees such epistemological philosophy as anthropocentric, since human knowledge is at the center of concern. Epistemological philosophy as the central focus is disguised anthropocentrism. Ecocentric philosophy would place knowledge of the relation of humans within their world at the forefront, and knowledge of the interaction of the diverse parts of a habitat functioning in a whole. But more, it would replace epistemological speculations with moral wisdom, in working out the place of a destructive species in its own environment. Human knowledge is within and a response to environments. Only by interacting with our environment can knowledge arise; all knowledge is knowledge of elements of the environment in some respect.

Europe in particular has acted against the interests of the ecology and environmental interests. During the twelfth and thirteenth centuries, populations all over Europe gradually increased, rising from around thirty six million in 1000 to about eighty million in 1300, stimulating the reclamation of arable and pasture lands from surrounding forests and wetlands. In 1000, the peninsulas and islands of Europe (Italy, Spain, Portugal, Denmark, the Netherlands, and the British Isles) had been about 5–10 percent forested; in France, Germany, and Austria a quarter of the land was in forests; and in central Europe and Scandinavia one to two-thirds of the land was forested. As towns grew, food surpluses produced in the countryside to feed townspeople increased pressure on arable lands, stimulating additional forest clearing. The heavy plow, invented in the sixth century, and the three-field system of agriculture, introduced in France around 800, spread across Europe during the ensuing centuries. The three-field system left one-third of the arable land fallow each year, while wheat, rye, oats, barley, and peas were rotated on the remaining two-thirds. Nature's unpredictability in the form of droughts, freezes, cold winters, storms, and climate variations often meant food shortages and famines. In many regions, soils became eroded and exhausted of nutrients.

Pasture and marginal soils were brought into production. By 1300, forest cover had dramatically declined over much of Europe. From the mid-fourteenth to the mid-fifteenth centuries, outbreaks of bubonic plague—another of nature's unpredictable actors—decimated populations. The "Black Death," so terrible in scope for the human populace, temporarily restored much of the land's fecundity. Forests grew back renewing timber supplies, marshes returned, and soils recovered fertility. Yet environmental recovery was short-lived as the European population again increased (from approximately ninety million in 1600 to around two hundred million in 1800). Population pressure was coupled with a new phenomenon—mercantile capitalism— that reshaped European land and life beginning in the sixteenth century.

An inexorably expanding market economy, which arose in the city states of Renaissance Italy and spread gradually to northern Europe, intensified medieval tendencies toward capitalism. Stimulated by the European discovery and exploitation of the Americas, the spreading use of money facilitated open-ended accumulation. Cities flourished as centers of trade and handicraft production, giving rise to a new class of bourgeois entrepreneurs. These new businessmen supplied ambitious monarchs with the funds and expertise to build strong nation-states, and their rise undercut the power of the landowning nobility. As commerce and trade expanded, forests were cut for lumber and charcoal, and cleared lands were turned into pastures. Between 1650 and 1750, large tracts of forested lands were cleared for agriculture and industry. Shipbuilding; tanning; glass, and soap making; and tin, lead, copper, and iron mining and smelting helped denude the forest cover. Swamps were drained, mine shafts sunk, and ore extracted from the "bowels of the earth." Streams were polluted, fish killed, and fields fouled with runoff. Everywhere, early capitalist development altered the landscape. In 1700, European land use comprised 230 million hectares of forests and woodlands, 190 million hectares of pasture lands, and 67 million hectares of croplands. By 1850, forests and wood lands had declined to 205 million hectares, while pasture had risen to 150 million hectares and croplands to 132 million hectares.

The emerging bourgeoisie adopted a new secular narrative that legitimated the changes wrought on the earth. Capitalism's origin story moves from desert wilderness to cultivated garden. In the new story, undeveloped nature is transformed into a state of civility, producing a reclaimed Garden of Eden. The wild is tamed, wilderness subdued. The Recovery of Eden Narrative is the story into which most Westerners have been socialized and within which we live our lives today. This story is one of converting wilderness into ordered civil society— creating a reinvented Eden— through science, technology, and capitalism.

In the sixteenth century, the most palpable forms of undeveloped nature were forests and wastes. Wild places were synonymous with uncultivated, uninhabited forests, wastes, and deserts. While woodlots on the edges of towns and fields were known and used, deep forests were dark and unknown—places in which one might become bewildered and lost. Wastes were open, unused lands with little vegetation. "Wilde" and "wylde" pertained to untamed animals living in a state of nature and to uncultivated, undomesticated plants. "Wild" persons were viewed as savage, uncivilized, rude, uncultured, licentious, unruly, and unpredictable.

Tales of wilderness in European and Anglo-Saxon folklore were dramatized by fifteenth- and sixteenth-century explorations of the New World. The "savages" of the new lands became symbols of the wildness and animality that could gain the upper hand in "civilized" persons. As European elite culture set itself increasingly above nature as represented by its own medieval past and by New World "savagery," a code of manners was adopted that advocated the suppression of beastlike qualities in humans and the transformation of wildness into civility.

Knowing the habits of the "savages" of North America enabled elite Europeans to characterize themselves as civilized and their own society as civil. The voyages of discovery and descriptions of America by New World colonists were used to define the meaning of wild and by extension the meaning of "civilized." Persons living in the "state of nature" were presumed to be lawless. Wild men, it was argued, had no laws, religion, property, or manners. In his *Natural and Moral History of the Indies* (1604), Joseph de Acosta asserted that the first men to inhabit the Indies were "savage men and hunters," who then "bred up" into "civill and well governed Common-weales." In 1609, Garcilaso de la Vega observed that New World natives "lived like wild beasts without religion, nor government, nor towns, nor houses, without tilling or sowing the soil, or clothing or covering their flesh Like wild beasts they ate the herbs of the field and roots of trees and fruits growing wild and also human flesh."

The 1607 settlement of Jamestown in North America engendered mixed reactions concerning Indians. In 1609, a Virginia colonist found people who lived "like herds of deer in the forest." Indians were seen as being as "wilde" as "wilde beasts." While some accounts portrayed Indians as happy in the state of nature, "courteous, gentle of disposition" and "civil and merry," the Virginia Massacre of 1622 that killed many of the Jamestown colonists, reinforced European fears of Indians as wild, brutish, and savage. Indians, like nature, could be chaotic and unpredictable. Contributing to the perception of nature as an unruly and lawless place therefore were human experiences of the deep forest, biblical accounts of the desert as wilderness, the witch trials of the sixteenth and early seventeenth centuries, and perceptions of New World peoples as wild and savage. Such factors pointed to the need to restore order to society and nature.

The idea of nature as a lawless place was reinforced by the apparent decay in the cosmos itself. By the late sixteenth century, the medieval worldview of a hierarchically ordered, immutable cosmos was breaking down. The hierarchy of the heavens, that moved upward from the earth to the moon, through the seven spheres of planets, to the fixed stars and empyrean heaven, was challenged by the work of Copernicus (1473–1543). His 1543 book *On the Revolutions of the Heavenly Spheres* placed the sun in the center of the cosmos and removed the earth to the third sphere. Tycho Brahe's (1546–1601) observations of a new star in the heavens in 1572 and of comets blazing across the sphere of the fixed stars introduced the idea of corruptibility and decay in the cosmos. In 1609, Johannes Kepler's (1571–1630) *New Astronomy* demonstrated that the planets moved in elliptical orbits, challenging the notion of perfectly circular paths. Galileo Galilei's (1564–1642) observations with the telescope in the *Sidereal Messenger* (1610) showed the moon to have craters, the sun to have spots, Jupiter to have moons, and Venus to have phases. To elite Europeans, these observations reinforced biblical notions that the decay of nature had been introduced into the world by the Fall of Man.

Godfrey Goodman's *The Fall of Man,* published in 1616, carried the theme of death and decay a step further. In the Fall from Eden, humanity not only introduced death to itself, but to all of nature. The parts of man and of nature had all declined from a perfect state of youth to old age, decay, and ultimately death. The Fall introduced decay into the human body, or microcosm, which in turn produced corruption in the larger world, or macrocosm. The decay of nature was evidenced by the decline of fish in the seas, infertility in the soils, and corruption in the heavens themselves (such as spots on the moon and comets that marred the perfection of the heavenly spheres). That nature needed repair, Goodman held, was shown by the development of technology While the ancients had not needed agriculture, living as they did in a state of abundance, the moderns, who were in a state of decline, needed it to restore the lost fertility of nature.

Other writers concurred that the Fall of Man had introduced death and decay into nature itself. The seventeenth-century poet Henry Vaughan (1622–95) wrote that man "drew the Curse upon the world, and Cracked the whole frame with his fall." Henceforth, he "sighed for Eden" and longed "for home." In *Paradise Lost* (1668), John Milton (1608–74) wrote that when Eve ate the apple, "Earth felt the wound, and Nature from her seat,/Sighing through all her works, gave signs of woe." The earth "trembled from her entrails," "Nature gave a second groan," and the sky "wept at completing of the mortal Sin Original." But for some writers, the idea of nature's decay was set within a larger story of cyclical decay, followed by the rebirth of the earth.

Thomas Burnet's *Sacred Theory of the Earth* (1684) presented an epic narrative of the decline of the earth. The story began with the Creation, and proceeded to the Fall, and then the decay, and conflagration of the entire world. The destruction, however, ended with the subsequent rebirth of the earth, thus holding out hope of regaining paradise. Like the Christian Edenic and Greek golden-age theories, Burnet's narrative began with a perfect earth in perpetual spring, lapsed into a fall and period of decay, out of which it entered a new period of rebirth and rejuvenation. The earth, Burnet believed, was formed out of chaos with the four elements all in their proper spheres, earth at the center, water on the surface, air above, and fire beyond. The original earth was "smooth, regular, and uniform; without Mountains, and without a Sea." The earth known by Adam and Eve was one of perfection, as befitted a paradise. After the fall from Eden came the Great Flood, initiating decay throughout the entire surface of the once perfect earth. In the flood, the "Earth was broken and swallowed up," and "Nature seem'd to be in a second Chaos." Storms raged on the seas; forests and cities were drowned. The irregular, malformed earth that resulted was the earth of the present era.

The next stage of the earth, Burnet predicted, would be its conflagration. The fire would begin in Rome, seat of the Antichrist. After the burning ceased, paradise would be reproduced and the thousand-year reign of Christ on earth would begin. A second race of men would then arise on the new earth. This "new Order of Nature" would last until the new race rose in final conflict destroying Satan, at which time the Saints would rise to heaven, and the earth itself would become a fixed star. At that point the "whole Circle of Time and Providence" would be completed.

During the seventeenth century, the Christian narrative of dominion over nature was combined with science, technology, and capitalist development to reinforce the possibility of remaking the earth as a controlled, managed Garden of Eden. Social values of order and control paved the way toward acceptance of a new narrative of dominion over nature. The mechanical worldview created by the "fathers of modern science" drew on philosophical assumptions consistent with the power of machine technologies to control the natural world. Early capitalist development was based on watermills, windmills, furnaces, forges, cranes, and pumps that transformed and multiplied the energy of sun, wind, wood, and coal to produce ships, guns, cannons, ammunition, cloth, paper, planks, flour, glass, and a myriad of iron implements and utensils. The large pumping, milling, and lifting machines found everywhere in daily life made plausible a model of nature as a machine. The cosmos was likened to a clock that regulated time in equal units. God was depicted as a clockmaker, mathematician, and engineer who constructed and directed the world from outside.

For Descartes, motion was not inherent in the corpuscles themselves, but was put into the world by God at the beginning of the cosmic story and transferred from one particle to another. God sustained the created world from instant to instant throughout time. Owing to God's immutable intellect, the laws of nature were both unchanging and intelligible to the human mind. The external (extended) world of nature was described in terms of measurable quantities such as size, weight, and speed. The internal world of the mind was the source of clear and distinct ideas—the basis for truth. The logic underlying the mathematical method was the key to valid knowledge of the external world. Mathematical descriptions of the material world were the ground of certainty and yielded the laws of nature. In his *Discourse on Method* (1637), Descartes argued that through knowing the forces of bodies we could "render ourselves the masters and possessors of nature." By the late seventeenth century, Christianity's idea of dominion over nature had merged with science, technology, and capitalism to form the secular, mainstream narrative. According to Carolyn Merchant:

> "*The acquisition of private property was the key to humanity's progress from the "state of nature"*

> *into ordered civil society. As early as 1625, Dutch statesman Hugo Grotius (1583–1645) maintained that private property had been created through stages of development when "common ownership, first of movable objects, later also of immovable property, was abandoned." In 1651 English Philosopher Thomas Hobbes's (1588–1679) Leviathan described the "state of nature" as a place in which there were no arts or letters and where civil society itself could not even exist. (74)"*

Movements like Romanticism and Transcendentalism emerged to counter the destructive effects wrought by Cartesian principles and anthropocentrism. Romanticism and Transcendentalism were at the forefront in reviving the ties with the ecology. While Cartesianism and anthropocentrism aimed at dominating the ecology and non-human nature through a mechanistic and scientific approach, Romanticism and Transcendentalism adopted a holistic approach designed to reconcile the human community with the ecology.

Rachel Carson's *Silent Spring* was instrumental in reviving environmental and ecological concerns during the 20th century. She was critical of the use of pesticides and insecticides and her work illustrated the disastrous consequences resulting from the use of chemicals in the agricultural industry. The concerns expressed by Rachel Carson were taken up by other environmentalists and philosophers who called for a re-examination of the human-nature relationship. Philosophy and ecology began to be clubbed together for a sustainable earth and a better future.

Deep Ecology movement emerged more or less spontaneously and informally as a philosophical and scientific social/political movement during the so-called Ecological Revolution of the r96os. Its main concern has been to bring about a major paradigm shift-a shift in perception, values, and lifestyles-as a basis for redirecting the ecologically destructive path of modern industrial growth societies. Since the r96os, the long-range Deep Ecology movement has been characterized philosophically by a move from anthropocentrism to ecocentrism, and by environmental activism.

The philosophical roots of the Deep Ecology movement are found in the ecocentrism and social criticism of Henry David Thoreau, John Muir, D. H. Lawrence, Robinson Jeffers, and Aldous Huxley. Influential ecological/social criticism has been also derived from the writings of George Orwell and Theodore Roszak, and from the critiques of the problems created by the rise of civilizations written by the maverick historian Lewis Mumford. Further inspiration for contemporary ecological consciousness and the Deep Ecology movement can be traced to the ecocentric religions and ways of life of primal people around the world, and to Taoism, Saint Francis of Assisi, the Romantic Nature-oriented countercultural movement of the nineteenth century with its roots in Spinoza, and the Zen Buddhism of Alan Watts and Gary Snyder.

Professional philosophers began to explore the immense philosophical implications raised by the environmental crisis in the late 1960s. For example, Arne Naess first began lecturing and writing on "Philosophy and Ecology" at the University of Oslo in 1968 and later at the University of Hong Kong in 1972 As long-time chairman of the philosophy department at the University of Oslo, and as a result of the influence of his books on semantics and the history of philosophy in the Norwegian school system, Naess's name has been nearly synonymous with philosophy in Norway for over fifty years. At a Third World Futures conference held in Bucharest in 1972, Naess pointed out that two environmental movements had arisen during the 1960s: a "shallow" anthropocentric technocratic environmental movement concerned primarily with pollution, resource depletion, and "the health and affluence of people in the developed countries," and an ecocentric "Deep, Long-Range Ecology movement". Since first coining the term in 1972, Naess has continued to develop and refine the Deep Ecology position to the present day.

The Pulitzer Prize-winning poet and essayist Gary Snyder also worked out a unique Deep Ecological position beginning in the 1960s. Together with fellow Californians Peter Berg and the ecologist Raymond Dasmann, Snyder has developed the foundations for ecocentric bioregionalism. Snyder has had an immense impact for over twenty-five years on the rise of the Deep Ecology movement. He and Naess are its two most influential international exponents. Naess's "shallow/ Deep Ecology" distinction was largely unknown outside Scandinavia until the 1980s, when it began to receive widespread attention among philosophers and environmentalists. Worldwide awareness of the Deep Ecology movement resulted, in large part, from the publication of Deep Ecology by Bill Devall and George Sessions in 1985, and as a result of the publicity arising from the ecological activist group Earth First! throughout the 1980s.

Deep Ecology based on ecological philosophy was based on reverence and coexistence between the human community and the ecology. Similar ideas have been expressed by the myths and religious beliefs of various communities. Despite being marginalized and treated as a part of the minority traditions during the colonial era, the native cultures of Asia, Africa and America have sustained the ecological philosophy through their myths, cultural practices and religious beliefs. In fact, they acted as a foil to the anthropocentrism of the West.

A closer study of the myths, legends, folklore and cultural practices reveals a deeply ingrained reverence for the natural world and ecology- something that stands in contrast with the exploitive attitude of the European imperial powers. Environmental concerns are growing with each passing day, and the myths of the bygone days hold the sacred wisdom that had sustained the human-nature relationship in the past and could do so in the future.

Prologue

Will you teach your children what we have taught our children? That the earth is our mother? What befalls the earth befalls all the sons of the earth. This we know: the earth does not belong to man, man belongs to the earth. All things are connected like the blood that unites us all. Man did not weave the web of life, he is merely a strand in it. Whatever he does to the web, he does to himself. One thing we know: our god is also your god. The earth is precious to him and to harm the earth is to heap contempt on its creator.

-Chief Seattle

CHAPTER ONE

THE WORLD OF MYTHS

Human beings have always been mythmakers. Archaeologists have unearthed Neanderthal graves containing weapons, tools and the bones of a sacrificed animal, all of which suggest some kind of belief in a future world that was similar to their own. The Neanderthals may have told each other stories about the life that their dead companion now enjoyed. They were certainly reflecting about death in a way that their fellow-creatures did not. Animals watch each other die but, as far as we know, they give the matter no further consideration. But the Neanderthal graves show that when these early people became conscious of their mortality, they created some sort of counter-narrative that enabled them to come to terms with it. The Neanderthals who buried their companions with such care seem to have imagined that the visible, material world was not the only reality. From a very early date, therefore, it appears that human beings were distinguished by their ability to have ideas that went beyond their everyday experience.

A peculiar characteristic of the human mind is its ability to have ideas and experiences that we cannot explain rationally. We have imagination, a faculty that enables us to think of something that is not immediately present, and that, when we first conceive it, has no objective existence. The imagination is the faculty that produces religion and mythology. Today mythical thinking has fallen into disrepute; we often dismiss it as irrational and self-indulgent. But the imagination is also the faculty that has enabled scientists to bring new knowledge to light and to invent technology that has made us immeasurably more effective. The imagination of scientists has enabled us to travel through outer space and walk on the moon, feats that were once only possible in the realm of myth. Mythology and science both extend the scope of human beings.

Mythology speaks of another plane that exists alongside our own world, and that in some sense supports it. Belief in this invisible but more powerful reality, sometimes called the world of the gods, is a basic theme of mythology. It has been called the 'perennial philosophy' because it informed the mythology, ritual and social organisation of all societies before the advent of our scientific modernity, and continues to influence more traditional societies today. According to the perennial philosophy, everything that happens in this world, everything that we can hear and see here below has its counterpart in the divine realm, which is richer, stronger and more enduring than our own.

And every earthly reality is only a pale shadow of its archetype, the original pattern, of which it is simply an imperfect copy. It is only by participating in this divine life that mortal, fragile human beings fulfil their potential. The myths gave explicit shape and form to a reality that people sensed intuitively. They told them how the gods behaved, not out of idle curiosity or because these tales were entertaining, but to enable men and women to imitate these powerful beings and experience divinity themselves.

Mythology was therefore designed to help us to cope with the problematic human predicament. It helped people to find their place in the world and their true orientation. We all want to know where we came from, but because our earliest beginnings are lost in the mists of prehistory, we have created myths about our forefathers that are not historical but help to explain current attitudes about our environment, neighbours and customs. We also want to know where we are going, so we have devised stories that speak of a posthumous existence – though, as we shall see, not many myths envisage immortality for human beings. And we want to explain those sublime moments, when we seem to be transported beyond our ordinary concerns. The gods helped to explain the experience of transcendence. The perennial philosophy expresses our innate sense that there is more to human beings and to the material world than meets the eye.

Since the eighteenth century, we have developed a scientific view of history; we are concerned above all with what actually happened. But in the premodern world, when people wrote about the past they were more concerned with what an event had meant. A myth was an event which, in some sense, had happened once, but which also happened all the time. Because of our strictly chronological view of history, we have no word for such an occurrence, but mythology is an art form that points beyond history to what is timeless in human existence, helping us to get beyond the chaotic flux of random events, and glimpse the core of reality.

The simplest and most direct way to approach mythology is to look at its subject matter. In the broadest terms myths are traditional stories about gods, kings, and heroes. Myths often relate the creation of the world and sometimes its future destruction as well. They tell how gods created men. They depict the relationships between various gods and between gods and men. They provide a moral code by which to live. And myths treat the lives of heroes who represent the ideals of a society. In short, myths largely deal with the significant aspects of human and superhuman existence.

It is easy to forget this in reading about the many absurd, barbaric, comic, grotesque, or sentimental occurrences in various mythologies. Yet, on the whole, myths have a certain dignity and eloquence precisely because they do grapple with important matters. Myths are generally stories that have been handed down for generations, popular tales that embody a collective knowledge. While some may have originated with shamans, priests, or poets, myths belong to a primitive or pre-scientific people as their cultural heritage.

Usually, they have been shaped by the folk imagination. Very often myths are accepted as the literal truth. They are not presented as engaging fictions but as fact. Even in the sophisticated, intelligent culture of classical Greece myths were frequently viewed as actualities. And when they were regarded sceptically writers reshaped them to make them more probable and humane.

Forget for the moment that the myths of other cultures are considerably more bizarre and savage. It must seem incredible to us, conditioned as we are by materialism and scientific rationality, that the ancient Greeks for the most part could take seriously a philandering deity like Zeus, an incredible hero like Perseus, or a monster like the Medusa. It would seem to presuppose much ignorance and gullibility. However, the primary appeal of myth is to the imagination, to man's intuitive faculty. In a society where reason is poorly developed or non-existent, the imagination is the only arbiter of truth. And even where reason is predominant, as it was in classical Greece, the imagination still exerts a strong hold on one's beliefs. A culture, after all, can never abandon its age-old traditions without undergoing disintegration.

In their vital stage, when they are accepted as truth, myths represent the learning of a society, its accumulated knowledge and wisdom. Any body of myths tries to give a comprehensive account of the world and of the people to whom it belongs. It does this through narrative, through memorable stories that deal with matters that perplex and intrigue primitive man. The crude mythology of an Australian tribe; the priestly mythologies of Egypt, Babylonia, and India; the liberating mythology of Greece and Rome; and the heroic mythology of Scandinavia offer a way of apprehending reality, of making sense of nature and human life, no matter how irrational they might appear to us. Every mythology has its obscurities, inconsistencies, and absurdities, but the crucial point is that myths attempt to give form to the cosmos and meaning to human life. We shall see this ordering impulse in each of the mythologies in this volume.

Most modern scholars divide the subject into three principal categories: pure myth, heroic saga, and the folk tale. Pure myth is both primitive science and primitive religion. It consists of stories that explain natural phenomena such as the sun, stars, flowers, storms, volcanoes, and so on, or of stories that show how men should behave toward gods. These myths recount how the world came into being, who the various gods are and what powers they control, how these gods affect the world and men, and the means by which men can propitiate these powers.

Gods can be personified natural agents such as fire, sky, earth, water, and the like. But more often they are beings that use specific areas of nature to effect their purposes, just as men operate machines to produce some end. Gods are often visualized as having human shape, feeling human emotions, and performing human acts, even if they are immortal and infinitely more powerful than men. This renders the cosmos more intelligible than it would be if it were ruled by impersonal, capricious forces that were indifferent to man's welfare. Gods, even at their cruellest, are much preferable to stark chaos. And gods that look and act as human beings do make the world appear more bearable, because they sanctify human beauty and strength by giving them supernatural precedent.

In interpreting nature, myths use analogical reasoning, relating the unfamiliar to the familiar by means of likeness. Thus, things in heaven happen the same way they do here on earth. Why does the sun move across the sky? Because some deity is pushing it, riding it, or sailing it through the universe each day. And just as beasts and men beget progeny by copulation, so the primordial elements of nature procreate on each other in most mythologies. Or to give another example, the ancient Greeks must have wondered why the constellations of Ursa Major and Ursa Minor never set below the horizon, whereas other groups of stars did. The mythological solution, related by Ovid in his tale of Callisto, is that they were outcasts. Hera hated those stars and ordered the sea never to let them sink, since they were once the living mistress and son of Hera's mate, Zeus. This shows mythological reasoning and the projection of human feelings onto the natural world.

A coordinate branch of myth deals with the art of getting the gods to effect human purposes. This involves primitive religion with a technological overcast. The gods, having some human qualities, may respond to worship, ritual, supplication, and sacrifice. They are never obliged to help human beings, but they can if they so desire. Gods sometimes show partiality by rewarding a few mortals with good fortune. But generally, nature is incalculable. One can never tell where lightning will strike, storms sink ships, wars and plagues ravage, earthquakes wreck cities, or flood, drought, and hail ruin crops. Yet psychologically a man is never totally impotent if he has gods to whom he can appeal. Myths frequently deal with the tributes one should pay a god, the chief of which is piety.

Yet there is an older, darker region of myth involving magic. Magic is also an attempt to influence the gods to fulfil human wishes. The Greeks pretty much expurgated or transmuted this element in their myths, but it has a fairly sizable place in the myths of primitive peoples and in the ancient Near Eastern and European mythologies.

Magic seeks to influence nature by imitation, by mimicking the results one wants. It depends upon analogical thought, whereby like produces like. The savage rite of human sacrifice was supposed to guarantee a plentiful harvest in Neolithic societies, because the sprinkling of human blood on the ground would bring the necessary rain to the crops.

In ancient cults throughout the Near East and Europe magic was associated with the worship of the triple-goddess, usually in agricultural communities presided over by a matriarchal queen. The triple-goddess stood for the three phases of the moon waxing, full, and waning; the three phases of nature planting, harvest, and winter; and the three phases of womanhood virgin, mature woman, and crone. In her earthly incarnation as queen, she often took a male lover each year, and when his period was through, he was ritually murdered. Traces of this archaic religion can be found in Greek mythology, but the Greeks with their patriarchal worship of Zeus managed to suppress it fairly thoroughly.

While men might use religious ritual or magic to induce the gods to grant their requests, it was extremely dangerous to antagonize a supernatural force. The gods were invariably ruthless in punishing acts of impiety or overweening pride. King Ixion, for attempting to ravish the goddess Hera, was struck dead by Zeus's thunderbolt, lashed to a turning wheel in hell, and bitten eternally by snakes. In the *Gilgamesh* epic the mighty Enkidu contracted a fatal illness for insulting Ishtar, the Babylonian fertility goddess. Dozens of myths vividly portray the folly and dire results of neglecting or provoking the gods. This is equally a matter of morality and of influencing nature.

In addition to explaining natural phenomena as the work of gods and showing how men should relate to these powers, myths can explain other things, such as the source and meaning of some ritual. A sacred rite can be impressive in itself, satisfying man's need for comforting repetition in an all-too-unstable world. But myth adds a spiritual dimension to ritual and gives it supernatural sanction. The story of Demeter and Persephone gave a transcendent significance to the Eleusinian rites. And Hesiod, in his tale of how Prometheus tricked Zeus, gave divine precedent to the fact that men get the hide and meat of a sacrificial animal while the gods get the fat and bones.

Myths can also account for the origin of names, whether of places or peoples. The story of Helle falling off the ram with the golden fleece into the sea explains how the Hellespont got its name. Icarus, of course, fell into the Icarian Sea after flying too close to the sun. The legend of Ion tells of the founder of the Ionian race, who also gave his name to the Ionian Sea. And the tale of Zeus creating a formidable race of men from an ant heap explains how Achilles' warriors, the Myrmidons, got their name, since *myrmex* is the Greek word for ant. Fanciful as they are, these stories made ancient geography and racial inheritance more intelligible to a people whose origins were in the remote and misty past.

Myths always express man's need to be aware of his roots. An important part of any mythology is the genealogy of gods, kings, and heroes. The lordly families of Homeric and post-Homeric Greece traced their ancestry to the legendary heroes of the Trojan War heroes who in turn traced their ancestry back to the gods. The scrupulous attention paid to genealogical lines in myths all over the world stresses that mythical and legendary figures were not created out of the blue but had distinguished blood lines behind them. Even the gods had parents in the cruder, primal elements of nature. Here again in myth divine processes reflect human processes and interests. If pure myth is explanatory, the heroic saga is often a primitive version of history. The saga condenses and dramatizes lengthy historical events into epic encounters. When Schliemann excavated and discovered the site of Troy in 1870, he lent some credence to the legend of the Trojan War. Archaeological evidence has established that a brilliant civilization flourished around the Aegean Sea from about 1500 to 1260 B.C., and that this Mycenaean culture was destroyed by the Dorian invasions, which threw Greece into the dark ages for four centuries. If the actual Trojan War took place with even half the magnitude that Homer describes, Asia Minor and Mycenaean Greece must have been considerably weakened, preparing the way for the Dorian invasions.

Later Greece saw the fall of Troy as the victory of Hellenism over the barbarian East, but it was hardly a victory if the foregoing is true. Yet peoples may rewrite legends to suit themselves. In fact, legends sometimes serve as propaganda to support an existing social structure, as the tale of Theseus was used by Euripides to bolster the faltering Athenian democracy in the Peloponnesian War. A legend is not infrequently a political tool to give added weight to some faction. And here we come to the most important function of heroic saga that of establishing a grand past for a people and setting forth the values by which a race is to live. Heroic legends embody the values of a society and orient the individual toward the standards and goals of his culture. They show what manhood consists of and how a great man lives and dies. In doing so they give meaning and direction to life.

Some modern theories of myth hail from the hoary disciplines of philosophy and literature, but they, too, reflect the influence of the social sciences. Each discipline harbours multiple theories of myth. Strictly, theories of myth are theories of some much larger domain, with myth a mere subset. For example, anthropological theories of myth are theories of culture *applied* to the case of myth. Psychological theories of myth are theories of the mind. Sociological theories of myth are theories of society. There are no theories of myth itself, for there is no discipline of myth in itself. Myth is not like literature, which, so it has or had traditionally been claimed, must be studied as *literature* rather than as history, sociology, or something else nonliterary. There is no study of myth as myth.

What unites the study of myth across the disciplines are the questions asked. The three main questions are those of origin, function, and subject matter. By 'origin' is meant why and how myth arises. By 'function' is meant why and how myth persists. The answer to the why of origin and function is usually a need, which myth arises to fulfil and lasts by continuing to fulfil. What the need is, varies from theory to theory. By 'subject matter' is meant the referent of myth. Some theories read myth literally, so that the referent is the straightforward, apparent one, such as gods. Other theories read myth symbolically, and the symbolized referent can be anything.

Theories differ not only in their answers to these questions but also in the questions they ask. Some theories, and perhaps some disciplines, concentrate on the origin of myth; others, on the function; still others, on the subject matter. Only a few theories address all three questions, and some of the theories that address origin or function deal with either 'why' or 'how' but not both.

It is commonly said that theories of the nineteenth century focused on the question of origin and that theories of the twentieth century have focused on the questions of function and subject matter. But this characterization confuses historical origin with recurrent origin. Theories that profess to provide the origin of myth claim to know not where and when myth first arose but why and how myth arises wherever and whenever it does. The issue of recurrent origin has been as popular with twentieth-century theories as with nineteenth-century ones, and interest in function and subject matter was as common to nineteenth-century theories as to twentieth-century ones.

There is one genuine difference between nineteenth- and twentieth-century theories. Nineteenth-century theories tended to see the subject matter of myth as the natural world and to see the function of myth as either a literal explanation or a symbolic description of that world. Myth was typically taken to be the 'primitive' counterpart to science, which was assumed to be wholly modern. Science rendered myth not merely redundant but outright incompatible, so that moderns, who by definition are scientific, had to reject myth. By contrast, twentieth-century theories have tended to see myth as almost anything but an outdated counterpart to science, either in subject matter or in function. Consequently, moderns are not obliged to abandon myth for science.

Besides the questions of origin, function, and subject matter, questions often asked about myth include: is myth universal? Is myth true? The answers to these questions stem from the answers to the first three questions. A theory which contends that myth arises and functions to explain natural processes will likely restrict myth to societies supposedly bereft of science. By contrast, a theory which contends that myth arises and functions to unify society may well deem myth acceptable and perhaps even indispensable to all societies.

A theory which maintains that myth functions to explain natural processes is committed to the falsity of myth if the explanation given proves incompatible with a scientific one. A theory which maintains that myth functions to unify society may circumvent the issue of truth by asserting that society is unified when its members *believe* that the laws they are expected to obey were established long ago by revered ancestors, whether or not those laws really were established back then. This kind of theory sidesteps the question of truth because its answers to the questions of origin and function do. According to Robert E Segal:

> "*That myth, whatever else it is, is a story may seem self-evident. After all, when asked to name myths, most of us think first of stories about Greek and Roman gods and heroes. Yet myth can also be taken more broadly as a belief or credo – for example, the American 'rags to riches myth' and the American 'myth of the frontier'. Horatio Alger wrote scores of popular novels illustrating the rags to riches myth, but the credo itself does*

not rest on a story. The same is true of the myth of the frontier. (4)"

If, then, myth is to be taken here as a story, what is the story about? For folklorists above all, myth is about the creation of the world. In the Bible only the two creation stories (Genesis 1 and 2), the Garden of Eden story (Genesis 3), and the Noah story (Genesis 6–9) would thereby qualify as myths. All the other stories would instead constitute either legends or folk tales. Outside the Bible the Oedipus 'myth', for example, would actually be a legend. According to Mircea Eliade:

"*Most of the Greek myths were recounted, and hence modified, adjusted, systematized, by Hesiod and Homer, by the rhapsodes and the mythographers. The mythological traditions of the Near East and of India have been sedulously reinterpreted and elaborated by their theologians and ritualists. This is not to say, of course, that (1) these Great Mythologies have lost their "mythical substance" and are only "literatures" or that (2) the mythological traditions of archaic societies were not rehandled by priests and bards. Just like the Great Mythologies that were finally transmitted as written texts, the "primitive" mythologies, discovered by the earliest travellers, missionaries, and ethnographers in the "oral" stage, have a "history." In other words, they have been transformed and enriched in the course of the ages under the influence of higher cultures or through the creative genius of exceptionally gifted individuals. (4)*"

For theories from, above all, religious studies, the main characters in myth must be gods or near-gods. Here, too, I do not propose being so rigid. If I were, I would have to exclude most of the Hebrew Bible, in which all the stories may *involve* God but, apart from only the first two chapters of Genesis, are at least as much about human beings as about God. I will insist only that the main figures be personalities – divine, human, or even animal. Excluded would be impersonal forces such as Plato's Good. Among theorists, E.B. Tylor is the most preoccupied with the personalistic nature of myth, but all the other theorists to be discussed assume it – with the exception of Levi-Strauss. At the same time the personalities can be either the agents or the objects of actions.

In other words, myth tells how, through the deeds of Supernatural Beings, a reality came into existence, be it the whole of reality, the Cosmos, or only a fragment of reality-an island, a species of plant, a particular kind of human behaviour, an institution. Myth, then, is always an account of a "creation"; it relates how something was produced, began to be. Myth tells only of that which really happened, which manifested itself completely. The actors in myths are Supernatural Beings. They are known primarily by what they did in the transcendent times of the "beginnings." Hence myths disclose their creative activity and reveal the sacredness (or simply the "supernaturalness") of their works. In short, myths describe the various and sometimes dramatic breakthroughs of the sacred (or the "supernatural") into the World. It is this sudden breakthrough of the sacred that really establishes the World and makes it what it is today.

We may add that in societies where myth is still alive the natives carefully distinguish myths-"true stories"-from fables or tales, which they call "false stories." The Pawnee "differentiate 'true stories' from 'false stories,' and include among the 'true' stories in the first place all those which deal with the beginnings of the world; in these the actors are divine beings, supernatural, heavenly, or astral. Next come those tales which relate the marvellous adventures of the national hero, a youth of humble birth who became the saviour of his people, freeing them from monsters, delivering them from famine and other disasters, and performing other noble and beneficent deeds. Last come the stories which have to do with the world of the medicine-men and explain how such-and such a sorcerer got his superhuman powers, how such-and-such an association of shamans originated, and so on. The 'false' stories are those which tell of the far from edifying adventures and exploits of Coyote, the prairie-wolf. Thus, in the 'true' stories we have to deal with the holy and the supernatural, while the 'false' ones on the other hand are of profane content, for Coyote is extremely popular in this and other North American mythologies in the character of a trickster, deceiver, sleight-of-hand expert and accomplished rogue." Similarly, the Cherokee distinguish between sacred myths (Cosmogony, creation of the stars, origin of death) and profane stories, which explain, for example, certain anatomical or physiological peculiarities of animals. The same distinction is found in Africa. The Herero consider the stories that relate the beginnings of the different groups of the tribe "true" because they report facts that really took place, while the more or less humorous tales have no foundation. As for the natives of

Togo, they look on their origin myths as "absolutely real." Eliade adds:

> "*Whereas "false stories" can be told anywhere and at any time, myths must not be recited except during a period of sacred time (usually in autumn or winter, and only at night). This custom has survived even among peoples who have passed beyond the archaic stage of culture. Among the Turco-Mongols and the Tibetans the epic songs of the Gesar cycle can be recited only at night and in winter. "The recitation is assimilated to a powerful charm. It helps to obtain all sorts of advantages, particularly success in hunting and war. ... Before the recitation begins, a space is prepared by being powdered with roasted barley flour. The audience sit around it. The bard recites the epic for several days. They say that in former times the hoofprints of Gesar's horse appeared in the prepared space. Hence the recitation brought the real presence of the hero." (10)*"

This distinction made by natives between "true stories" and "false stories" is significant. Both categories of narratives present "histories," that is, relate a series of events that took place in a distant and fabulous past. Although the actors in myths are usually Gods and Supernatural Beings, while those in tales are heroes or miraculous animals, all the actors share the common trait that they do not belong to the everyday world. Nevertheless, the natives have felt that the two kinds of "stories" are basically different. For everything that the myths relate concerns them directly, while the tales and fables refer to events that, even when they have caused changes in the World, have not altered the human condition as such.

Myths, that is, narrate not only the origin of the World, of animals, of plants, and of man, but also all the primordial events in consequence of which man became what he is today- mortal, organized in a society, obliged to work in order to live, and working in accordance with certain rules. If the world exists, if man exists, it is because Supernatural Beings exercised creative powers in the "beginning." But after the cosmogony and the creation of man other events occurred, and man as he is today is the direct result of those mythical events, he is constituted by those events. He is mortal because, something happened in *illo tempore*. If that thing had not happened, man would not be mortal-he would have gone on existing indefinitely, like rocks; or he might have changed his skin periodically like snakes, and hence would have been able to renew his life, that is, begin it over again indefinitely. But the myth of the origin of death narrates what happened in *illo tempore*, and, in telling the incident, explains why man is mortal.

To analyse a myth is to analyse it from the viewpoint of some theory. Theorizing is inescapable. For example, handbooks of classical mythology that matter-of-factly connect Adonis' annual trek to Persephone and return to Aphrodite with the course of vegetation presuppose a view of myth as the primitive counterpart to science. Being sceptical of the universality of any theory is one thing. Being able to sidestep theorizing altogether is another.

Theories need myths as much as myths need theories. If theories illuminate myths, myths confirm theories. True, the sheer applicability of a myth does not itself confirm the theory, the tenets of which must be established in their own right. For example, to show that Jung's theory, when applied, elucidates the myth of Adonis would not itself establish the existence of a collective unconscious, which, on the contrary, would be presupposed. But one, albeit indirect, way of confirming a theory is to show how well it works *when* its tenets are assumed – this on the grounds that the theory must be either false or limited if it turns out not to work. Mircea Eliade explains:

> "*In general it can be said that myth, as experienced by archaic societies, (1) constitutes the History of the acts of the Supernaturals; (2) that this History is considered to be absolutely true (because it is concerned with realities) and sacred (because it is the work of the Supernaturals); (3) that myth is always related to a "creation" it tells how something came into existence, or how a pattern of behavior, an institution, a manner of working were established; this is why myths constitute the paradigms for all significant human acts; (4) that by knowing the myth one knows the "origin" of things and hence can control and manipulate them at will; this is not an "external," "abstract" knowledge but a knowledge that one "experience" ritually, either by: ceremonially recounting the myth or by performingthe ritual for which it is the justification; (5) that in one way or another one*

"lives" the myth, in the sense that one is seized by the sacred exalting power of the events recollected or re-enacted. (18-19)"

"Living" a myth, then, implies a genuinely "religious" experience, since it differs from the ordinary experience of everyday life. The "religiousness" of this experience is due to the fact that one re-enacts fabulous, exalting, significant events, one again witnesses the creative deeds of the Supernaturals; one ceases to exist in the everyday world and enters a transfigured, auroral world impregnated with the Supernaturals' presence. What is involved is not a commemoration of mythical events but a reiteration of them. The protagonists of the myth are made present, one becomes their contemporary. This also implies that one is no longer living in chronological time, but in the primordial Time, the Time when the event first took place. This is why we' can use the term the "strong time" of myth; it is the prodigious, "sacred" time when something new, strong, and significant was manifested. To reexperience that time, to re-enact it as often as possible, to witness again the spectacle of the divine works, to meet with the Supernaturals and relearn their creative lesson is the desire that runs like a pattern through all the ritual reiterations of myths.

To approach myth from the field of religious studies is naturally to subsume myth under religion but is thereby to expose myth to the challenge to religion from science. Twentieth-century theories from religious studies have sought to reconcile myth with science by reconciling religion with science.

There have been two main strategies for reconciling the two. One tactic has been to re-characterize the subject matter of religion and therefore of myth. Religion, it has been argued, is not about the physical world, in which case religion is safe from any encroachment by science. The myths considered under this approach to religion are traditional myths, such as biblical and classical ones, but they are now read symbolically rather than literally.

The other tactic has been to elevate seemingly secular phenomena to religious ones. As part of this elevation, myth is no longer confined to explicitly religious ancient tales. There are now overtly secular modern myths as well. For example, stories about heroes are at face value about mere human beings, but the humans are raised so high above ordinary mortals as to become virtual gods. At the same time the actions of these 'gods' are not supernatural and are thus not incompatible with science. This approach retains a literal reading of myth but re-categorizes the literal status of the agents in myth.

There is a third tactic: replacing religious myths with secular ones. This strategy saves myth from the fate of religion by severing myth from religion. It is thus the opposite of the second tactic: turning secular myths into religious ones.

Myth is commonly taken to be words, often in the form of a story. A myth is read or heard. It says something. Yet there is an approach to myth that deems this view of myth artificial. According to the myth and ritual, or myth-ritualist, theory, myth does not stand by itself but is tied to ritual. Myth is not just a statement but an action. The least compromising form of the theory maintains that all myths have accompanying rituals and all rituals accompanying myths. In tamer versions some myths may flourish without rituals or some rituals without myths. Alternatively, myths and rituals may originally operate together but subsequently go their separate ways. Or myths and rituals may arise separately but subsequently coalesce. Whatever the tie between myth and ritual, the myth-ritualist theory differs from other theories of myth and from other theories of ritual in focusing on the tie.

The myth-ritualist theory was pioneered by the Scottish Biblicist and Arabist William Robertson Smith (1846–94). In his *Lectures on the Religion of the Semites* Smith argues that belief is central to *modern* religion but not to *ancient* religion, in which ritual was central. Smith grants that ancients doubtless performed rituals only for some reason. But the reason was secondary and could even fluctuate. And rather than a formal declaration of belief, or a creed, the reason was a story, or a *myth*, which simply described 'the circumstances under which the rite first came to be established, by the command or by the direct example of the god'.

The relationship between myth and literature has taken varying forms. The most obvious form has been the use of myth in works of literature. A standard theme in literature courses has been the tracing of classical figures, events, and themes in Western literature thereafter – beginning with the Church Fathers, who utilized classical mythology even while warring on paganism, and proceeding through Petrarch, Boccaccio, Dante, Chaucer, Spenser, Shakespeare, Milton, Goethe, Byron, Keats, and Shelley, and then down to Joyce, Eliot, Gide, Cocteau, Anouilh, and Eugene O'Neill. The same has commonly been done for biblical myths. Both groups of myths have alternatively been read literally, been read symbolically, been rearranged, and been outright recreated. And they are to be found in all of the arts, including music and film. Freud used the figures Oedipus and Electra to name the most fundamental human drives, and he took from psychiatrists the figure Narcissus to name self-love.

The pervasiveness of classical, or pagan, mythology is even more of a feat than that of biblical mythology, for classical mythology has survived the demise of the religion of which, two thousand years ago, it was originally a part. By contrast, biblical mythology has been sustained by the near-monolithic presence of the religion of which it remains a part. Indeed, classical mythology has been preserved by the culture tied to the religion that killed off classical religion.

In *From Ritual to Romance* the English medievalist Jessie Weston (1850–1928) applied Frazer's second myth-ritualist version to the Grail legend. Following Frazer, she maintains that for ancients and primitives alike the fertility of the land depended on the fertility of their king, in whom resided the god of vegetation. But where for Frazer the key ritual was the replacement of an ailing king, for Weston the aim of the Grail quest was the *rejuvenation* of the king. Furthermore, Weston adds an ethereal, spiritual dimension that transcends Frazer. The aim of the quest turns out to have been mystical oneness with god and not just food from god. It is this spiritual dimension of the legend that inspired T. S. Eliot to use Weston in 'The Waste Land'. Weston is not reducing the Grail legend to primitive myth and ritual but merely tracing the legend back to primitive myth and ritual. The legend itself is literature, not myth. Because Frazer's second myth-ritualist scenario is not about the enactment of any myth of the god of vegetation but about the condition of the reigning king, the myth giving rise to the legend is not the life of a god like Adonis but the life of the Grail king himself.

In *The Idea of a Theater* Francis Fergusson (1904–86), an esteemed American theatre critic, applied Frazer's second myth-ritualist version to the whole genre of tragedy. He argues that the story of the suffering and redemption of the tragic hero derives from Frazer's scenario of the killing and replacement of the king. For example, Oedipus, King of Thebes, must sacrifice his throne, though not his life, for the sake of his subjects. Only with his abdication will the plague cease. But for Fergusson, as for Weston, the renewal sought is less physical than spiritual, and for Fergusson, Oedipus seeks it for himself as well as for his people. More than most other literary myth-ritualists, Fergusson is concerned as much with the product – drama – as with the source – myth and ritual. He even criticizes Harrison and especially Murray for taking the meaning of tragedy to be the Frazerian act of regicide rather than, say, the theme of self-sacrifice. For Fergusson, as for Weston, the Frazerian scenario provides the background to literature but is itself myth and ritual rather than literature.

In *Anatomy of Criticism* famed Canadian literary critic Northrop Frye (1912–91) argued that not one genre but all genres of literature derive from myth – specifically, the myth of the life of the hero. Frye associates the life cycle of the hero with several other cycles: the yearly cycle of the seasons, the daily cycle of the sun, and the nightly cycle of dreaming and awakening. The association with the seasons comes from Frazer. The association with the sun, never attributed, perhaps comes from Max Muller. The association with dreaming comes from Jung. The association of the seasons with heroism, while again never attributed, may come from Raglan, who will shortly be considered in his own right. Frye offers his own heroic pattern, which he calls the 'quest-myth', but it consists of just four broad stages: the birth, triumph, isolation, and defeat of the hero. Each main genre of literature parallels at once a season, a stage in the day, a stage of consciousness, and above all a stage in the heroic myth. Romance parallels at once spring, sunrise, awakening, and the birth of the hero. Comedy parallels summer, midday, waking consciousness, and the triumph of the hero. Tragedy parallels autumn, sunset, daydreaming, and the isolation of the hero. Satire parallels winter, night, sleep, and the defeat of the hero. The literary genres do not merely parallel the heroic myth but derive from it. The myth itself derives from ritual – from the version of Frazer's myth-ritualism in which divine kings are killed and replaced.

Like most other literary myth-ritualists, Frye does not reduce literature to myth. On the contrary, he, most uncompromisingly of all, insists on the autonomy of literature. Like Fergusson, he faults Murray and Cornford not for speculating about the myth-ritualist origin of tragedy (Murray) and comedy (Cornford) – a non-literary issue – but for interpreting the meaning of both as the enactment of Frazer's scenario of regicide – the literary issue.

In *Violence and the Sacred* and other works Rene Girard, whose theory was discussed in the previous chapter, offers the sharpest break between myth and literature. Like Fergusson and Frye, Girard faults Harrison and Murray for conflating myth and ritual with tragedy. But he faults the two even more sternly for domesticating tragedy. For Harrison and Murray, myth merely *describes* the Frazerian ritual, and tragedy merely *dramatizes* it. Worse, tragedy turns an actual event into a mere theme. For Girard, myth *covers up* the ritual, and tragedy, as in Sophocles' plays about Oedipus, *uncovers* it. Girard's criticism, however, is directed at Frazer's second myth-ritualist scenario, in which the king is outright killed. Harrison and Murray use instead Frazer's first myth-ritualist scenario, in which the king merely plays the part of the god of vegetation. In that scenario the god dies but the king does not, and the god may die without being killed, as in Adonis' annual trek to Hades. Girard's charge that Harrison, Murray, and even in part Frazer miss the human killing that underlies all tragedy is thus embarrassingly misdirected.

Another aspect of myth as literature has been the focus on a common story line. Nowhere in Tylor or Frazer is there any consideration of myth as story. It is not that either Tylor or Frazer would deny that a myth is a story. It is, rather, that both deem myth a causal explanation of events that merely happens to take the form of a story.

The parallel of myth to science requires the downplaying of the story form and the playing up of the explanatory content. Of course, myth for both tells the 'story' of how Helios becomes responsible for the sun and how he exercises that responsibility, but what interests Tylor and Frazer is the information itself, not the way it is conveyed. Standard literary considerations, such as characterization, time, voice, point of view, and reader response, are ignored, just as they would be in the analysis of a scientific law.

Because myth for Tylor and Frazer is intended to explain recurrent events, it could be rephrased as a law. For example: Whenever rain falls, it falls because the god of rain has decided to send it, and always for the same reason. When the sun rises, it rises because the sun god has chosen to mount his chariot, to which the sun is attached, and to drive the chariot across the sky, and again always for the same reason. Insofar as Frazer takes the gods to be symbols of natural processes, myth rephrased would be merely descriptive and not explanatory: it would simply be saying *that* rain falls (regularly or not) or *that* the sun rises (regularly) but not *why*. For Tylor in particular, who reads myth literally, myth is anything but literature, and to approach myth as literature is to trivialize it, to turn its explanatory truth claims into elaborate poetic descriptions. Where Frye and others argue that literature is not reducible to myth, Tylor argues that myth is not reducible to literature. In the wake of postmodernism, in which arguments in all fields, including science and law, are re-characterized as stories, Tylor's indifference to the story aspect of myth is notable.

Tylor's separation of myth from story is no less notable when seen from the standpoint of the American literacy critic Kenneth Burke (1897–1993). In, above all, *The Rhetoric of Religion* Burke argues that myth is the transformation of metaphysics into story. Myth expresses symbolically, in terms of temporal priority, what *primitives* cannot express literally: metaphysical priority. In Burke's famous phrase, myth is the 'temporizing of essence'.

Myths collectively are too varied to share a plot, but common plots have been proposed for specific kinds of myths, most often for hero myths. Other categories of myths, such as creation myths, flood myths, myths of paradise, and myths of the future, have proved too disparate for all but the broadest commonalities. Tylor specifies only that myths tell how a god decides to cause a natural event, but not what the god is like or how the god acts. Narrowing his focus to gods of vegetation, Frazer specifies only that they die and are reborn, not how either occurs. Back in 1871 Tylor, surprisingly turning briefly from myths about gods to hero myths, argued that in many hero myths the subject is exposed at birth, is saved by other humans or animals, and grows up to become a national hero. Tylor sought only to establish a common pattern, not to apply to hero myths his theory of the origin, function, and subject matter of myths generally.

In 1876 the Austrian scholar Johann Georg von Hahn used fourteen cases to argue that all 'Aryan' hero tales follow an 'exposure and return' formula more comprehensive than Tylor's. In each case the hero is born illegitimately, out of the fear of the prophecy of his future greatness is abandoned by his father, is saved by animals and raised by a lowly couple, fights wars, returns home triumphant, defeats his persecutors, frees his mother, becomes king, founds a city, and dies young. Though himself a solar mythologist, von Hahn, like Tylor, tried only to establish a pattern for hero myths. Had he proceeded to theorize about the tales, his theory would have rested on the commonality of the plot.

Similarly, in 1928 the Russian folklorist Vladimir Propp sought to demonstrate that Russian fairy tales follow a common plot, in which the hero goes off on a successful adventure and upon his return marries and gains the throne. Propp's pattern skirts both the birth and the death of the hero. While himself a Marxist, Propp here, in his earlier, formalist phase, attempted no more than Tylor and von Hahn: to establish a pattern for hero stories. But again, any theoretical salvo would have depended on the commonality of the plot.

Where for Tylor and Frazer myth deals exclusively, or nearly exclusively, with physical phenomena – flooding, disease, death – for Bronislaw Malinowski myth deals even more with social phenomena – marriage, taxes, and, ritual. Myth still serves to reconcile humans to the unpleasantries of life, but now to unpleasantries that, far from unalterable, *can* be cast off. Myths spur resigned acceptance by tracing these unpleasantries – or at least impositions – back to a hoary past, thereby conferring on them the clout of tradition.

Myth persuades denizens to defer to, say, ranks in society by pronouncing those ranks long-standing and in that sense deserved. A myth about the British monarchy would make the institution as ancient as possible, so that to tamper with it would be to tamper with tradition. In England today fox hunting is defended on the grounds that it has long been part of country life. Social myths say, 'Do this because this has always been done.' In the case of physical phenomena the beneficiary of myth is the individual. In the case of social phenomena the beneficiary is society itself.

To say that myth traces back the origin of phenomena is equivalent to saying that myth explains those phenomena. When, then, Malinowski, railing against Tylor, declares that primitives 'do not want to "explain," to make "intelligible" anything which happens in their myths', he is really asserting that myths are not, as for

Tylor, explanations for their own sake. Yet explanations they must still be, for only by explaining phenomena do they serve their conciliatory function.

There is no escaping our dependence on myth. Without it, we cannot determine what things are, what to do with them, or how to be in relation to them. The fundamental structures of understanding that myths provide, even though in part dictated by matter and instinct, are nevertheless essentially arbitrary because they describe not just the "real" world of "fact" but our perception and experience of that world.

While all cultures have specific myths through which they respond to these kinds of questions, it is in their creation myths that the most basic answers are to be found. Not only are creation myths the most comprehensive of mythic statements, addressing themselves to the widest range of questions of meaning, but they are also the most profound. They deal with first causes, the essences of what their cultures perceive reality to be. In them people set forth their primary understanding of man and the world, time and space. And in them cultures express most directly, before they become involved in the fine points of sophisticated dogma, their understanding of and awe before the absolute reality, the most basic fact of *being*.

The cultural and religious nature of the myths narrating the creation of man, the world and other life forms often treat the natural world and the ecology as sacred. Myths and religious traditions have created a deeply ingrained belief in the sacredness of the ecology. When people talk about religion, most soon mention the major religious traditions of our times. But then, thinking further, most mention as well the religions of indigenous peoples and of such vanished civilizations as ancient Greece and Egypt and Persia. That is, we have come to understand that there are—and have been—many different religions; anthropologists estimate the total in the thousands. They also estimate that there have been thousands of human cultures, which is to say that the making of a culture and the making of its religion go together: Every religion is embedded in its cultural history. As each culture evolves, a unique Cosmos and Ethos appear in its co-evolving religion. For billions of us, back to the first humans, the stories, ceremonies, and art associated with our religions-of-origin are central to our matrix.

A cosmology works as a religious cosmology only if it resonates, only if it makes the listener feel religious. To be sure, the *beauty* of Nature—sunsets, woodlands, fireflies—has elicited religious emotions throughout the ages. We are moved to awe and wonder at the grandeur, the poetry, the richness of natural beauty; it fills us with joy and thanksgiving. Our response to accounts of the *workings* of Nature, on the other hand, is decidedly less positive. The scientific version of how things are, and how they came to be, is much more likely, at first encounter, to elicit alienation, anomie, and nihilism, responses that offer little promise for motivating our allegiance or moral orientation.

We live in a world densely populated by humans in close communication with one another over the surface of the earth. More and more, the world looks like a single society, a "global village." But in fact, human society consists of a great many groups, as different from one another as the city dwellers of New York, rice farmers of India, and aboriginal hunters of northern Canada. People of our global village differ not only in their daily occupations and material wealth, but also in the ways in which they view the world around them. This multitude of perceptions is directly related to cultural diversity around the world, a diversity that is rapidly shrinking. Surrounded by the built landscape, it has become difficult for many people to relate to the environment. This alienation from nature has contributed to the environmental problems of the contemporary world. But at the same time, it has triggered a search for new ways of relating to nature.

Myths and religious beliefs have represented the voice of nature to humanity. Spiritual teachings have celebrated and consecrated our ties to the nonhuman world, reminding us of our delicate and inescapable partnership with air, land, water, and fellow living beings. To assess religion's view of nature—and to see how contemporary theology deals with the environmental crisis—we must therefore attend with care to the full range of writings and practices which religious traditions offer.

CHAPTER TWO

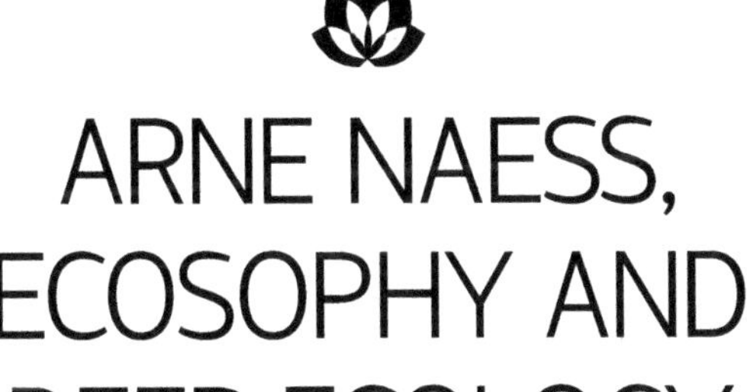

ARNE NAESS, ECOSOPHY AND DEEP ECOLOGY

Awe, reverence, love, and affection along with fear, frustration, and grudging respect have long marked human beings' attitude toward the natural world. In recent years the ethical and religious attitude of valuing nature for its own sake and seeing it as divine or spiritually vital has been called "Deep Ecology." The simple and overwhelming reason why a new name is needed for a human attitude that may be tens of thousands of years old is that history has fundamentally altered our relationship to the surrounding, supporting Earth. Deep ecology has emerged as a response to what we have done to nature. According to David Barnhill and Roger Gottlieb:

> "*Having altered the atmosphere by thinning the ozone, affected global weather patterns, extinguished species at a rate unknown for tens of millions of years and consciously created new ones, we have put an end to that relatively*

> *autonomous realm. Of course every breath, hut building, and berry picking alters "nature." But the global effects of what we have done over the last century or so are monumentally larger than anything we might have even dreamed of before. Even if we think of "nature" as including human beings, we find that one part of nature—ourselves—is having vastly disproportionate and unsettling effects on the other parts. (1)*"

But deep ecology embodies more than a love of and identification with nature, and a simple recognition that all of us, whether or not we flee from it in denial, live in the midst of an environmental crisis. It also purports to be the guiding philosophy of an environmental movement that seeks to slow or halt the ruin. Other philosophical or religious values guided wars of conquest or rebellion, shaped movements for national liberation or racial justice. Similarly, a renewed reverence for wilderness, endangered species can stem the rot.

As have the rise of science, the struggle for democracy, and recent challenges to racism, the environmental crisis will alter religious sensibilities. It has already called forth explicit proclamations from almost every established religion. Whether nature is considered valuable in itself or as a part of God's creation, most religious authorities now see it as deserving of care, stewardship, and respect. In this way traditional religions are making (perhaps unconscious) common cause with deep ecologists and their kindred: radical environmentalists, ecofeminists, witches, and various tree-huggers of indeterminate self-description.

Further, religious rituals, from church services in honour of animals to Buddhist meditations emphasizing our interdependence with the natural world, have been and will continue to be created and practiced. Considered as a technology of spiritual life, rituals allow us to celebrate even in the midst of devastation, and to express a kind of formalized, collective contrition for our ecological sins. As methods of focusing spiritual energy and moral intention, rituals are essential to a religious life that seeks to be more than a purely inner experience. Spiritual imagination and creativity are needed to continue to help us find widely meaningful ways to allow us to do this. Finally, religions need to face how the environmental crisis changes certain basic facts about the spiritual meaning of the world around us. Considered as God's creation, nature—at least in the form of the ecosystems that make up this current phase of earth's biological development— is now subject to human intervention, alteration, and (to some extent, at least) control. In the words of Katherine Keller and Laurel Kearns:

> "*Ecological difference pushes the encounter with the Other over the edge, into the infinity of nonhumans, into the engulfing differences of biodiversity. We may be accustomed in our philosophy or theology to an ancient stretch beyond the human, indeed beyond the earth's atmosphere. Nonetheless the present stretch, this self-extension into the full terrestrial spectrum of pressing, vulnerable life: this feels inhuman. We defer. We despair. We deny. We return to thought as usual. (2)*"

The recognition of the problem and its subsequent study using philosophical methods is called *Eco-philosophy*. More precisely, it is the utilisation of basic concepts from the science of ecology - such as complexity, diversity, and symbiosis - to clarify the place of our species within nature through the process of working out a total view.

The Norwegian philosopher and ecologist, Arne Naess has been one of the foremost champions of ecological philosophy. He used Ecosophy and Deep Ecology to offer solutions to the environmental and ecological crises. Ecosophy is derived from the word *ecology*, "the study of interrelationships," and *sophia*, "wisdom." *Ecosophy* is Naess's term for personal life philosophies aiming for ecological harmony. The philosophical side of Eco-philosophy investigates the particular methods of viewing the world that lead different individuals to something like the platform of deep ecology. Naess calls this reasoning process *ecosophy,* if it becomes articulated in a philosophical manner.

Deep ecology has emerged as a way of developing a new balance and harmony between individuals, communities and all of Nature. It can potentially satisfy our deepest yearnings: faith and trust in our most basic intuitions; courage to take direct action; joyous confidence to dance with the sensuous harmonies discovered through spontaneous, playful intercourse with the rhythms of our bodies, the rhythms of flowing water, changes in the weather and seasons, and the overall processes of life on Earth. About the process of Deep Ecology, George Sessions and Bill Devall explain:

> "*This is the work we call cultivating ecological consciousness. This process involves becoming*

more aware of the actuality of rocks, wolves, trees, and rivers - the cultivation of the insight that everything is connected. Cultivating ecological consciousness is a process of learning to appreciate silence and solitude and rediscovering how to listen. It is learning how to be more receptive, trusting, holistic in perception, and is grounded in a vision of nonexploitive science and technology. (8)"

This process involves being honest with ourselves and seeking clarity in our intuitions, then acting from clear principles. It results in taking charge of our actions, taking responsibility, practicing self-discipline and working honestly within our community. It is simple but not easy work. Henry David Thoreau, nineteenth-century naturalist and writer, admonishes us, "Let your life be a friction against the machine."

We believe that humans have a vital need to cultivate ecological consciousness and that this need is related to the needs of the planet. At the same time, humans need direct contact with untrammeled wilderness, places undomesticated for narrow human purposes. Many people sense the needs of the planet and the need for wilderness preservation. But they often feel depressed or angry, impotent and under stress. They feel they must rely on "the other guy," the "experts." Even in the environmental movement, many people feel that only the professional staff of these organizations can make decisions because they are experts on some technical scientific matters or experts on the complex, convoluted political process. But we need not be technical experts in order to cultivate ecological consciousness. Cultivating ecological consciousness, as Thoreau said, requires that "we front up to the facts and determine to live our lives deliberately, or not at all." We believe that people can clarify their own intuitions, and act from deep principles.

Deep ecology supporters appreciate the inherent value of all beings and of diversity. Therefore, research and communication should be inclusive and nonviolent. Th e ecological crisis, as driven by the modern model of industrial progress and human population growth, threatens the integrity of planetary ecosystems with their accumulated wealth of diverse forms of life, cultures, and worldviews. No single philosophy can solve all of these problems. Global progress requires broad cooperation at the level of collective action and common principles, with innovation and unique solutions at policy and local personal levels. Naess sees the deep ecology movement as one of many international grassroots liberation movements of the twentieth century for social justice, peace, and ecological responsibility (i.e., freedom from tyranny and inequity, from war and violence, from pollution of our bodies, and from the destruction of our home place).

For Naess, free nature is critical to cultural flourishing, community health, and personal self-realization. Personal, cultural, ecological, and evolutionary diversity are great treasures of the earth, probably even of cosmic significance. Th ere is room for a wide range of initiatives and actions to better care for and restore our shared home planet. Th e essays assembled in this book are devoted to Naess's work and his approach to complex global problems. As readers will see from this varied collection of his writings, Naess's interests, range over wide areas of scholarship and personal explorations, especially in the wild areas of the planet, intellect, and spirit. In his later years, he concentrated more and more on integrating his various interests and writings by means of a comprehensive, global approach using analytic, empirical, comparative, and other methods. All these and more are represented here and are organized by ecological issues and themes.

Naess turned his attention to environmental issues and Eco-philosophy during the 1960s. He read books by Rachel Carson, and her sense of wonder for nature inspired him to work on shifting to quality of life values and a nature-oriented sensibility that finds joy in the world of diverse beings. Carson's sense for the interconnected nature of the world and her scientific evaluation of the negative effects of massive herbicide and pesticide use are described in her book *Silent Spring* (1962). This turned him to thinking about the accelerating negative impacts on nature by contemporary industrial civilization and larger issues of ultimate aims and norms. His first foray into Eco-philosophy was in 1965 when he wrote a short essay, "Nature ebbing out". In the United States, the first Earth Day in 1970 was a historical landmark of the widespread concern over the accelerating destruction of nature by the forces of industrial society, rapid human population growth, and the rampant destruction of habitat for native species.

He presented his well-known seminal paper "The shallow and the deep, long-range ecology movement: A summary" in 1972 at an Eastern European conference on the future of research. In this paper, he describes the "shallow ecology movement" as an instrumental valuing of nature. It involves the "Fight against pollution and resource depletion. Central objective: the health and affluence of people in the developed nations." He said that this mainstream view is not a deep questioning approach. It assumes that we can go on with business as usual without deeply examining and changing our values and ultimate purposes. He describes the "deep ecology movement" as involving the recognition that we have to examine our basic relationships, values, and priorities with respect for each other and the natural world. Living beings are good for their own sake and have intrinsic value. This deep questioning approach leads us to see how our values, whether explicit or assumed, engender lifestyles that fail to honour our ecological responsibilities and the need for fundamental changes in industrial society. Ecologically based approaches involve "Rejection of the man-in-environment image in favour of the relational, total-field image." We are part of the larger ecological context and cannot stand outside it. We participate in it and affect it no matter what we do. It supports and affects us.

Naess says that the deep ecology movement is one of the three great international grassroots movements of the twentieth century; the other two are the peace and social justice movements. He says that while these movements should cooperate with each other, the ecology movement has a special responsibility for conversations with and conservation of nature. The relationship between what he calls "ultimate premises," "the platform of the deep ecology movement," and specific coalitions for social change can be encouraged between greens, social justice advocates, and the peace movement, as briefly described in the article on the "apron diagram." In that explanation, he makes clear that his study of the international ecology movement is connected to a larger appreciation for grassroots movements. He distinguishes between four levels of discourse when discussing these issues.

The level of everyday life assumes certain values in our ordinary practices. When we begin to seek deeper clarification of our ultimate values, we are involved in deep questioning that leads us to state our ultimate norms and views about the nature of the world. The three great international grassroots movements each have a number of principles of a general nature that serve as a uniting ground, even though these movements are supported by people from different nations, cultures, and religions who hold different ultimate philosophies. The four levels of discourse he describes are: ultimate philosophies, platform principles, policy formulations, and practical actions. There is great diversity at the level of ultimate philosophies but some unity at the level of platform principles. In the three great movements referred to above, there are platform principles that serve to unite people at the global level, although they have different personal philosophies and cultures. Policy and practical action are also more diverse since they are adapted to specific cultures, places, and individuals. Naess says that the ecology movement is enriched by this wonderful cultural diversity and that it is unwise to try to have only one ultimate philosophy or religion in the world. Instead, his vision is of a great diversity of cultures and ecosophies. Followers of the deep ecology movement are inspired to work together locally and globally to move our societies and personal lives toward sustainability. Naess is a celebrant of individual and cultural diversity, believing that this is nature's way and that these are all interdependent with ecological diversity.

Naess continually encourages people to consider their own way of living in the world, both in politics and in daily life. By focusing on positive emotions, we increase our freedom and sense of belonging to a larger world. While many other writers evoke despair and hopelessness in our contemporary situation, Naess emphasizes various forms of joy. We can find joy in watching small birds, walking among wildflowers, enjoying companionship with friends, family, and nature. In the face of continuing, daily assaults on wild places, he advises us to have "a sense of joy in a world of fact" to keep our balance and inspiration. One of his favorite slogans is "The front is very long." There is a place in the deep, long-range ecology movement for all people who share the desire to dwell responsibly in this world. People can contribute to the well-being of other human beings and of nature in a wide variety of ways, including doing beautiful actions. According to Naess:

> *"The deep ecology movement was, soon after The Silent Spring, made the object of studies, mostly from special viewpoints. It seems useful, however, to retain a conception that covers all aspects of the kind of achievement Rachel Carson was known for: primarily the warnings about man-made ecological disasters magnified through the involvement of industry and agriculture; secondarily the effort to implement new policies and personal activism; thirdly the philosophical and religious view of life and what makes life meaningful, especially as the basis for an*

environmentally alert ethics. (89)"

Deep ecology offers a philosophical basis for environmental advocacy which may, in turn, guide human activity against perceived self-destruction. Deep ecology and environmentalism hold that the science of ecology shows that ecosystems can absorb only limited change by humans or other dissonant influences. Further, both hold that the actions of modern civilization threaten global ecological well-being. Ecologists have described change and stability in ecological systems in various ways, including homeostasis, dynamic equilibrium, and "flux of nature". Regardless of which model is most accurate, environmentalists contend that massive human economic activity has pushed the biosphere far from its "natural" state through reduction of biodiversity, climate change, and other influences. As a consequence, civilization is causing mass extinction. Deep ecologists hope to influence social and political change through their philosophy.

The central spiritual tenet of deep ecology is that the human species is a part of the Earth and not separate from it. A process of self-realisation or "re-earthing" is used for an individual to intuitively gain an ecocentric perspective. The notion is based on the idea that the more we expand the self to identify with "others" (people, animals, ecosystems), the more we realize ourselves.

Central to the philosophy of deep ecology is the formation of what Naess calls a "total view" of the place of human beings in the world. A total viewwhat philosophers traditionally have termed a worldview combines our scientific understanding of reality with a valuation and emotional content, experience, or commitment. Naess writes that there are "two inescapable components" of deep ecology, the first being "valuation and emotion in thinking and experience of reality," and the second being "how they lead to the ability of a mature, integrated human personality to act on the basis of a total view." The total view, then, is essentially a normative description of reality, an understanding of the world that merges objective empirical observations and personal values. More specifically, a deep ecological total view would address the human relationship to the non-human natural world and connect this normative understanding directly to action; an individual's total view should be the basis of all decisions regarding his or her life.

A commitment to developing and living by a total view is, perhaps, the essential characteristic of deep ecology as it is positively differentiated from a shallow or reform environmentalism. Shallow environmentalism is labelled "shallow" precisely because it does not seek to work out a total view. The limitation of the shallow movement is not due to weak or unethical philosophy since it is often based on systematic utilitarian thinking and extensive economic cost-benefit analyses but due to a lack of explicit concern with ultimate aims, goals, and norms. Shallow environmentalism is characterized by decisions and policies that reflect merely partial understandings of reality and the human place in the natural world.

One of the limitations of shallow reformist environmentalism is that it does not take seriously the concerns, interests, or value of the nonhuman natural world. A deep ecological total view is not merely any type of total philosophical worldview, but a philosophical worldview that includes the nonhuman natural world, that includes the environment or the ecosphere in its normative understanding and value commitments. Because of the inclusion of the "ecosphere," a deep ecological worldview can be called an "ecosophy," a philosophical position or point of view that concentrates on the human relationship with the natural world.

The development of a philosophical worldview is the result of a personal commitment and individual thought and experience. Each individual must develop his or her own total view, a personal ecosophy to understand his or her place in the world. Each individual's ecosophy serves as the personal justification for principles of action in the environment and a deep ecological total view will incorporate the principles embodied in the deep ecology platform. Indeed, the development of each individual's ecosophy may be the principal goal of the philosophy of deep ecology.

Deep ecology is not one of many different environmental ethical theories, such as biocentric individualism or animal rights theory. It is, instead, a position in environmental *philosophy,* the philosophy of nature, the philosophy of human ecology, it is a *cosmology* or a *worldview,* and that may be the source of its depth. The advocates of deep ecology claim that the most important task is to understand the world in the right way; given the correct understanding, the ethical choices will be obvious. Naess argues that environmental disagreements are largely the result of different perceptions of reality. The developers of a forest see the forest differently than those who wish to preserve it. To solve real-world environmental problems, then, requires not the development of a new ethical theory but a new worldview, a new philosophy of the relationship between humanity and nature. According to Bill Devall and George Sessions:

> "*Cultivating ecological consciousness in contemporary societies, however, is a two-edged sword. We must not be misled by our zeal for change so that we are concerned only with the narrow self or ego. If we seek only personal redemption we could become solitary ecological saints among the masses of those we might classify as "sinners" who continue to pollute. Change in persons requires a change in culture and vice versa. We cannot ignore the personal arena nor the social, for our project is to enhance harmony with each other, the planet and ourselves. (14)*"

Healing the environment must begin in our own personal lives. We must examine our own choices and actions. Do the choices we make each day support the forces that are destructive to the environment? If so, we must commit ourselves to changing our choices, our habits, one by one. Nothing is too small to be overlooked. Everything we do counts, as far as its effect on the environment is concerned. What we eat, what we wear, what we buy, what we do for work or pleasure, everything must be weighed in the environmental balance.

For deep ecology, non-living entities and systems rivers, watersheds, landscapes, ecosystems are to be valued for their inherent value, not merely for their usefulness to humanity. Richness and diversity are also important values in the deep ecology platform, and here again these are thought to be valuable in themselves, and not merely as they contribute to human well-being. Naess and Rothenberg claim that an ecologically complex world is better than one that is less complex. "Complexity" is contrasted with "complication" it implies a unified diversity in nature, what Rothenberg calls ''the virtue and perfection of nature." Mere complication, on the other hand, is a chaotic "manifold" of alternative possibilities, built on false dualisms and dilemmas, with no overall purpose, plan, or unified structure. Rothenberg contrasts the development of natural entities and systems with the operations of machines to illustrate the distinction between complexity and complication. Human technology is complicated, but nature is complex, and it is this complexity its richness and diversity that ought to be preserved and valued for itself.

Given these primary concerns the value of living beings and natural systems and the preservation of a rich and diverse natural world it is obvious that a policy of non-interference in the natural world is advocated by the deep ecology platform. The human non-interference in the flourishing of natural systems is, of course, only an ideal human activities and institutions constantly interfere in the natural world in some way. But the supporters of deep ecology seek to minimize this interference, to preserve the unfolding of natural processes in all of their rich and diverse complexity. To maintain this policy of minimal interference, human society may have to be restructured thus deep ecology's controversial claims about the reduction of human population levels but the basic changes will come in the economic, technological, social, and philosophical bases of human civilization. Most important, perhaps, is a fundamental re-examination of the ends of human life, replacing the ceaseless pursuit of material abundance with a new sense of the quality of life experience. Thus we arrive at the simple, practical maxim of deep ecology: "simple in means, rich in ends."

The science of ecology, or at least one school of ecology that takes a broader holistic view, provides a new vision of the earth as a system of interconnected relationships. Emerging out of the discourse of ecology is a view of human society as part of a web of life within the ecosystem. This view is a radical departure from the static, mechanical, disembodied view of the world formulated by Descartes, Newton, and other thinkers of the Age of Enlightenment, and which has dominated our thinking. The land ethics of Aldo Leopold, Deep Ecology of Naess 1989, a sense of place, bioregionalism, topophilia or love of land, and biophilia or love of living things are some of the ways in which people concerned with environmental ethics have searched for the personal and spiritual element of ecology that has been missing in scientific ecology. Yet others have explored Eastern religions and Native American worldviews for insights. These efforts are very much a part of the broader context of the interest in traditional ecological knowledge, since it represents experience acquired over thousands of years of direct human contact with the environment.

For thousands of years, myths, legends, folklore and religious practices have shaped cultures and societies. Needless to say, myths also shaped the beliefs of the humans pertaining to the ecology and environmental practices. The myths helped the early human societies in building a close and intimate relationship with the natural world and at the same time made the humans aware of their position in the ecological system. The myths, legends and religious beliefs cultivated an awareness and respect among the humans for the nature; creation myths heavily made use of natural elements and phenomena to reinforce the importance of nature. The views articulated by Deep Ecology and Ecosophy in the 20th century, are very much similar to the views expressed by the various myths and religious practices from around the world. in those myths, legends and folklore, animals are vested with divine qualities and this rendered them sacred. The sacredness of animals and non-human nature went a long way in conserving the environment and built a sustainable and harmonious relationship between the humans and non-human nature.

Deep ecology goes beyond a limited piecemeal shallow approach to environmental problems and attempts to articulate a comprehensive religious and philosophical worldview. The foundations of deep ecology are the basic intuitions and experiencing of ourselves and Nature which comprise ecological consciousness.

Many of the questions are perennial philosophical and religious questions faced by humans in all cultures over the ages. What does it mean to be a unique human individual? How can the individual self-maintain and increase its uniqueness while also being an inseparable aspect of the whole system wherein there are no sharp breaks between self and the *other?* An ecological perspective, in this deeper sense, results in what Theodore Roszak calls "an awakening of wholes greater than the sum of their parts. in spirit, the discipline is contemplative and therapeutic."

Ecological consciousness and deep ecology are in sharp contrast with the dominant worldview of technocratic-industrial societies which regards humans as isolated and fundamentally separate from the rest of Nature, as superior to, and in charge of, the rest of creation. But the view of humans as separate and superior to the rest of Nature is only part of larger cultural patterns. For thousands of years, Western culture has become increasingly obsessed with the idea of *dominance:* with dominance of humans over nonhuman Nature, masculine over the feminine, wealthy and powerful over the poor, with the dominance of the West over non-Western cultures. Deep ecological consciousness allows us to see through these erroneous and dangerous illusions.

For deep ecology, the study of our place in the Earth household includes the study of ourselves as part of the organic whole. Going beyond a narrowly materialist scientific understanding of reality, the spiritual and the material aspects of reality fuse together. While the leading intellectuals of the dominant worldview have tended to view religion as "just superstition," and have looked upon ancient spiritual practice and enlightenment, such as found in Zen Buddhism, as essentially subjective, the search for deep ecological consciousness is the search for a more objective consciousness and state of being through an active deep questioning and meditative process and way of life.

Many people have asked these deeper questions and cultivated ecological consciousness within the context of different spiritual traditions-Christianity, Taoism, Buddhism, and Native American rituals, for example.

While differing greatly in other regards, many in these traditions agree with the basic principles of deep ecology. Bill Devall and George Sessions write:

> "*In keeping with the spiritual traditions of many of the world's religions, the deep ecology norm of self-realization goes beyond the modern Western self which is defined as an isolated ego striving primarily for hedonistic gratification or for a narrow sense of individual salvation in this life or the next. This socially programmed sense of the narrow self or social self dislocates us, and leaves us prey to whatever fad or fashion is prevalent in our society or social reference group. We are thus robbed of beginning the search for our unique spiritual/biological personhood. Spiritual growth, or unfolding, begins when we cease to understand or see ourselves as isolated and narrow competing egos and begin to identify with other humans from our family and friends to, eventually, our species. But the deep ecology sense of self requires a further maturity and growth, an identification which goes beyond humanity to include the nonhuman world. We must see beyond our narrow contemporary cultural assumptions and values, and the conventional wisdom of our time and place, and this is best achieved by the meditative deep questioning process. Only in this way can we hope to attain full mature personhood and uniqueness. (66-67)*"

A nurturing non-dominating society can help in the "real work" of becoming a whole person. The "real work" can be summarized symbolically as the realization of "self-in-Self' where "Self' stands for organic wholeness. This process of the full unfolding of the self can also be summarized by the phrase, "No one is saved until we are all saved," where the phrase "one" includes not only me, an individual human, but all humans, animals, birds, forest ecosystems, mountains and rivers, the tiniest microbes in the soil, and so on.

The intuition of biocentric equality is that all things in the biosphere have an equal right to live and blossom and to reach their own individual forms of unfolding and self-realization within the larger Self-realization. This basic intuition is that all organisms and entities in the ecosphere, as parts of the interrelated whole, are equal in intrinsic worth. Naess suggests that biocentric equality as an intuition is true in principle, although in the process of living, all species use each other as food, shelter, etc. Mutual predation is a biological fact of life, and many of the world's religions have struggled with the spiritual implications of this. Some animal liberationists who attempt to side-step this problem by advocating vegetarianism are forced to say that the entire plant kingdom including rain forests have no right to their own existence. This evasion flies in the face of the basic intuition of equality. Aldo Leopold expressed this intuition when he said humans are "plain citizens" of the biotic community, not lord and master over all other species.

Biocentric equality is intimately related to the all-inclusive Self-realization in the sense that if we harm the rest of Nature then we are harming ourselves. There are no boundaries and everything is interrelated. But insofar as we perceive things as individual organisms or entities, the insight draws us to respect all human and non-human individuals in their own right as parts of the whole without feeling the need to set up hierarchies of species with humans at the top.

In April 1984, during the advent of spring and John Muir's birthday, George Sessions and Arne Naess summarized fifteen years of thinking on the principles of deep ecology while camping in Death Valley, California. In this great and special place, they articulated these principles in a literal, somewhat neutral way, hoping that they would be understood and accepted by persons coming from different philosophical and religious positions. Bill Devall and George Sessions have outlined the basic principles:

> "*1. The well-being and flourishing of human and nonhuman Life on Earth have value in themselves (synonyms: intrinsic value, inherent value). These values are independent of the usefulness of the non-human world for human purposes.*
>
> *2. Richness and diversity of life forms contribute to the realization of these values and are also values in themselves.*
>
> *3. Humans have no right to reduce this richness and diversity except to satisfy vital needs.*
>
> *4. The flourishing of human life and cultures is compatible with a substantial decrease of the human population, The flourishing of nonhuman life requires such a decrease.*

> *5. Present human interference with the nonhuman world is excessive, and the situation is rapidly worsening.*
>
> *6. Policies must therefore be changed. These policies affect basic economic, technological, and ideological structures. The resulting state of affairs will be deeply different from the present.*
>
> *7. The ideological change is mainly that of appreciating life quality (dwelling in situations of inherent value) rather than adhering to an increasingly higher standard of living. There will be a profound awareness of the difference between big and great.*
>
> *8. Those who subscribe to the foregoing points have an obligation directly or indirectly to try to implement the necessary changes. (70)*"

The slogan of "non-interference" does not imply that humans should not modify some ecosystems as do other species. Humans have modified the earth and will probably continue to do so. At issue is the nature and extent of such interference.

The fight to preserve and extend areas of wilderness or near wilderness should continue and should focus on the general ecological functions of these areas (one such function: large wilderness areas are required in the biosphere to allow for continued evolutionary speciation of animals and plants). Most present designated wilderness areas and game preserves are not large enough to allow for such speciation.

Present ideology tends to value things because they are scarce and because they have a commodity value. There is prestige in vast consumption and waste (to mention only several relevant factors). Whereas "self-determination," "local community," and "think globally, act locally," will remain key terms in the ecology of human societies, nevertheless the implementation of deep changes requires increasingly global action- action across borders.

The essence of deep ecology is to ask deeper questions. The adjective 'deep' stresses that we ask why and how, where others do not. For instance, ecology as a science does not ask what kind of a society would be the best for maintaining a particular ecosystem – that is considered a question for value theory, for politics, for ethics. As long as ecologists keep narrowly to their science, they do not ask such questions. What we need today is a tremendous expansion of ecological thinking in what is called Ecosophy. *Sophy* comes from the Greek term *sophia,* 'wisdom,' which relates to ethics, norms, rules, and practice. Ecosophy, or deep ecology, then, involves a shift from science to wisdom.

For example, we need to ask questions like, Why do we think that economic growth and high levels of consumption are so important? The conventional answer would be to point to the economic consequences of not having economic growth. But in deep ecology, we ask whether the present society fulfils basic human needs like love and security and access to nature, and, in so doing, we question our society's underlying assumptions. We ask which society, which education, which form of religion, is beneficial for all life on the planet as a whole, and then we ask further what we need to do in order to make the necessary changes. We are not limited to a scientific approach; we have an obligation to verbalize a total view.

Of course, total views may differ. Buddhism, for example, provides a fitting background or context for deep ecology, certain Christian groups have formed platforms of action in favour of deep ecology, and I myself have worked out my own philosophy, which I call Ecosophy. In general, however, people do not question deeply enough to explicate or make clear a total view. If they did, most would agree with saving the planet from the destruction that's in progress. A total view, such as deep ecology, can provide a single motivating force for all the activities and movements aimed at saving the planet from human exploitation and domination.

Deep ecology is radically conservative in that it articulates a long-established minority stream of religion and philosophy in Western Europe, North America, and the. Orient. It also has strong parallels and shared insights with many religious and philosophical positions of primal peoples (including Native Americans). In a certain sense· it can be interpreted as remembering wisdom which men once knew.

While a great deal of modem literature has the anthropocentric focus of humans coping with urban lifestyles and their inherent problems, there is also a rich pastoral and naturalist literary tradition in Europe and America that provides a source for deep ecological consciousness. The European Romantic movement, beginning with Jean Jacques Rousseau's challenge to an overly civilized and refined Europe, and continuing with Goethe and the Romantic poets (Blake, Wordsworth, Coleridge, Shelley, etc.) can be viewed as a counterforce to the narrow scientism and industrialism of the modern world. This movement continued in America with Walt Whitman, the Transcendentalist Emerson, and Thoreau and Muir.

The major contribution of the science of ecology to deep ecology has been the rediscovery within the modern scientific context that everything is connected to everything else. Thus, as a science, ecology provided a view of Nature that was lacking in the discrete, reductionist approach to Nature of the other sciences.

Another contribution of the science of ecology was to encourage students to go into the field and really *see* interrelationships rather than just study them in textbooks or laboratories. Thus the scientist had to become a vital participant in the process. From the work of English pastor Gilbert White, through Thoreau, Muir, Charles Darwin, and others in the nineteenth century, to the more "radical" ecologists - Marston Bates, Frank Egler, Paul Ehrlich and others - ecologists have understood the need to go beyond the narrow definition of scientific data and look to their own consciousness to develop their own sense of place.

The guiding model for what a science should be from the seventeenth century onward has been physics. As architects of the Scientific Revolution, Rene Descartes and Isaac Newton envisioned the universe to be a gigantic machine explainable in simple linear cause-and-effect terms. According to Pierre LaPlace and others, it was just a matter of time before everything in the universe could be totally explained in these terms. The biological world could be explained by the principles of physics. The social sciences, including psychology and sociology, believed that in order to be respectable sciences, they too would have to model themselves after physics. The dominant Western metaphysics, from Democritus and Aristotle to the present, has viewed the world as a collection of discrete entities or substances. Modern physics was erected on this metaphysical view of reality as tiny bits of isolated matter- atoms. In addition, the objectivity of scientific knowledge was to be maintained by keeping the scientist distanced from what he was observing so that his emotions and subjective bias would not influence his findings.

Theoretical physicist Fritjof Capra in *The Tao of Physics* (1975) has done an outstanding job of explaining the revolution of the new physics and how this has resulted in a metaphysical view of reality similar to those of Eastern religions and ecological interrelatedness. In *The Turning Point* (1982), Capra carries this new view of metaphysical interrelatedness on to an examination of the changes which need to be made in our social structures. He suggests that deep ecology would be the appropriate framework for future human societies. In *The Turning Point* Fritjof Capra writes:

> "*Exploitation of nature has gone hand in hand with that of women, who have been identified with nature throughout the ages. From the earliest times, nature and especially the earth-was seen as a kind and nurturing mother, but also as a wild and uncontrollable female. In pre-patriarchal eras her many aspects were identified with the numerous manifestations of the Goddess. Under patriarchy the benign image of nature changed into one of passivity, whereas the view of nature as wild and dangerous gave rise to the idea that she was to be dominated by man. At the same time women were portrayed as passive and subservient to men. With the rise of*

Newtonian science, finally, nature became a mechanical system that could be manipulated and exploited, together with the manipulation and exploitation of women. The ancient association of woman and nature thus interlinks women's history and the history of the environment, and is the source of a natural kinship between feminism and ecology which is manifesting itself increasingly. (40-41)"

It is now becoming apparent that overemphasis on the scientific method and on rational, analytic thinking has led to attitudes that are profoundly anti-ecological. In truth, the understanding of ecosystems is hindered by the Very nature of the rational mind. Rational thinking is linear, whereas ecological awareness arises from an intuition of nonlinear systems. One of the most difficult things for people in our culture to understand is the fact that if you do something that is good, then more of the same will not necessarily be better. This, to me, is the essence of ecological thinking. Ecosystems sustain themselves in a dynamic balance based on cycles and fluctuations, which are nonlinear processes. Linear enterprises, such as indefinite economic and technological growth-or, to give a more specific example, the storage of radioactive waste over enormous time spans-will necessarily interfere with the natural balance and, sooner or later, will cause severe damage. Ecological awareness, then, will arise only when we combine our rational knowledge with an intuition for the nonlinear nature of our environment.

Such intuitive wisdom is characteristic of traditional, nonliterate cultures, especially of American Indian cultures, in which life was organized around a highly refined awareness of the environment. In the mainstream of our culture, on the other hand, the cultivation of intuitive wisdom has been neglected. This may be related to the fact that, in our evolution, there has been an increasing separation between the biological and cultural aspects of human nature. Biological evolution of the human species stopped some fifty thousand years ago. From then on, evolution proceeded no longer genetically but socially and culturally, while the human body and brain remained essentially the same in structure and size. In our civilization we have modified our environment to such an extent during this cultural evolution that we have lost touch with our biological and ecological base more than any other culture and any other civilization in the past. This separation manifests itself in a striking disparity between the development of intellectual power, scientific knowledge, and technological skills, on the one hand, and of wisdom, spirituality, and ethics on the other. Scientific and technological knowledge has grown enormously since the Greeks embarked on the scientific venture in the sixth century B.C. But during these twenty-five centuries there has been hardly any progress in the conduct of social affairs. Capra adds:

> "*Excessive self-assertion manifests itself as power, control, and domination of others by force; and these are, indeed, the patterns prevalent in our society. Political and economic power is exerted by a dominant corporate class; social hierarchies are maintained along racist and sexist lines, and rape has become a central*

> *metaphor of our culture rape of women, of minority groups, and of the earth herself. Our science and technology are based on the seventeenth-century belief that an understanding of nature implies domination of nature by "man." Combined with the mechanistic model of the universe, which also originated in the seventeenth century, and with excessive emphasis on linear thinking, this attitude has produced a technology that is unhealthy and inhuman; a technology in which the natural, organic habitat of complex human beings is replaced by a simplified, synthetic, and prefabricated environment. (44)"*

Before 1500 the dominant world view in Europe, as well as in most other civilizations, was organic. People lived in small, cohesive communities and experienced nature in terms of organic relationships, characterized by the interdependence of spiritual and material phenomena and the subordination of individual needs to those of the community. The medieval outlook changed radically in the sixteenth and seventeenth centuries. The notion of an organic, living, and spiritual universe was replaced by that of the world as a machine, and the world machine became the dominant metaphor of the modern era. This development was brought about by revolutionary changes in physics and astronomy, culminating in the achievements of Copernicus, Galileo, and Newton. The science of the seventeenth century was based on a new method of inquiry, advocated forcefully by Francis Bacon, which involved the mathematical description of nature and the analytic method of reasoning conceived by the genius of Descartes. Acknowledging the crucial role of science in bringing about these far-reaching changes, historians have called the sixteenth and seventeenth centuries the Age of the Scientific Revolution. One of the foremost figures of scientific thinking- Francis Bacon, called for radical and violent methods to subdues and subjugate nature.

The terms in which Bacon advocated his new empirical method of investigation were not only passionate but often outright vicious. Nature, in his view, had to be "hounded in her wanderings," "bound into service," and made a "slave." She was to be "put in constraint," and the aim of the scientist was to "torture nature's secrets from her." Much of this violent imagery seems to have been inspired by the witch trials that were held frequently in Bacon's time. As attorney general for King James I, Bacon was intimately familiar with such prosecutions, and because nature was commonly seen as female, it is not surprising that he should carry over the metaphors used in the courtroom into his scientific writings. Indeed, his view of nature as a female whose secrets have to be tortured from her with the help of mechanical devices is strongly suggestive of the widespread torture of women in the witch trials of the early seventeenth century. Bacon's work thus represents an outstanding example of the influence of patriarchal attitudes on scientific thought.

The ancient concept of the earth as nurturing mother was radically transformed in Bacon's writings, and it disappeared completely as the Scientific Revolution proceeded to replace the organic view of nature with the metaphor of the world as a machine. This shift, which was to become of overwhelming importance for the further development of Western civilization, was initiated and completed by two towering figures of the seventeenth century, Descartes and Newton.

The drastic change in the image of nature from organism to machine had a strong effect on people's attitudes toward the natural environment. The organic world view of the Middle Ages had implied a value system conducive to ecological behaviour. In the words of Carolyn Merchant:

> "*The image of the earth as a living organism and nurturing mother had served as a cultural constraint restricting the actions of human beings. One does not readily slay a mother, dig into her entrails for gold or mutilate her body, although commercial mining would soon require that. As long as the earth was considered to be alive and sensitive, it could be considered a breach of human ethical behavior to carry out destructive acts against it. For most traditional cultures, minerals and metals ripened in the uterus of the Earth Mother, mines were compared to her vagina, and metallurgy was the human hastening of the birth of the living metal in the artificial womb of the furnace-an abortion of the metal's natural growth cycle before its time. Miners offered propitiation to the deities of the soil and subterranean world, performed ceremonial sacrifices, and observed strict cleanliness, sexual abstinence, and fasting before violating the sacredness of the living earth by sinking a mine. Smiths assumed an awesome responsibility in precipitating the metal's birth through smelting, fusing, and beating it with*

hammer and anvil; they were often accorded the status of shaman in tribal rituals and their tools were thought to hold special powers. (3-4)"

The Renaissance image of the nurturing earth still carried with it subtle ethical controls and restraints. Such imagery found in a culture's literature can play a normative role within the culture. Controlling images operate as ethical restraints or as ethical sanctions- as subtle "oughts" or "ought-nots." Thus, as the descriptive metaphors and images of nature change, a behavioural restraint can be changed into a sanction. Such a change in the image and description of nature was occurring during the course of the Scientific Revolution.

Not only did the image of nature as a nurturing mother contain ethical implications but the organic framework itself, as a conceptual system, also carried with it an associated value system. Contemporary philosophers have argued that a given normative theory is linked with certain conceptual frameworks and not with others. The framework contains within itself certain dimensions of structural and normative variation, while denying others belonging to an alternative or rival framework.

Pastoral poetry and art prevalent in the Renaissance presented another image of nature as female-an escape backward into the motherly benevolence of the past. Here nature was a refuge from the ills and anxieties of urban life through a return to an unblemished Golden Age. Depicted as a garden, a rural landscape, or a peaceful fertile scene, nature was a calm, kindly female, giving of her bounty. Against an idyllic backdrop, sheep grazed contently, birds sang melodies, and trees bore fruit. Wild animals, thorns, snakes, and vultures were nowhere to be found. Human beings meditated on the beauties of nature far removed from the violence of the city.

But while the pastoral tradition symbolized nature as a benevolent female, it contained the implication that nature when ploughed and cultivated could be used as a commodity and manipulated as a resource. Nature, tamed and subdued, could be transformed into a garden to provide both material and spiritual food to enhance the comfort and soothe the anxieties of men distraught by the demands of the urban world and the stresses of the marketplace. It depended on a masculine perception of nature as a mother and bride whose primary function was to comfort; nurture, and provide for the wellbeing of the male. In pastoral imagery, both nature and women are subordinate and essentially passive. They nurture but do not control or exhibit disruptive passion. The pastoral mode, although it viewed nature as benevolent, was a model created as an antidote to the pressures of urbanization and mechanization. It represented a fulfilment of human needs for nurture, but by conceiving of nature as passive, it nevertheless allowed for the possibility of its use and manipulation. Unlike the dialectical image of nature as the active unity of opposites in tension, the Arcadian image rendered nature passive and manageable.

Shallow ecology is anthropocentric, or human-centered. It views humans as above or outside of nature, as the source of all value, and ascribes only instrumental, or "use," value to nature. Deep ecology does not separate humans--or anything else-from the natural environment. It sees the world not as a collection of isolated objects, but as a network of phenomena that are fundamentally interconnected and interdependent. Deep ecology recognizes the intrinsic value of all living beings and views humans as just one particular strand in the web of life.

Ultimately, deep ecological awareness is spiritual or religious awareness. When the concept of the human spirit is understood as the mode of consciousness in which the individual feels a sense of belonging, of connectedness, to the cosmos as a whole, it becomes clear that ecological awareness is spiritual in its deepest essence. It is, therefore, not surprising that the emerging new vision of reality based on deep ecological awareness is consistent with the so-called perennial philosophy of spiritual traditions.

CHAPTER THREE

THE CULT OF THE MOTHER GODDESS AND SACRED NATURE

At the root of every human culture are the stories we call myths—stories of the creation of the world and of humankind, of the deeds of gods and heroes, and of the end of time. Such stories explain and justify the world, and define our role within creation. Once a civilization has become established, the myths that formed it may dwindle into superstition or entertainment, but even so, they never lose their intrinsic power, for the world's mythologies enshrine all the poetry and passion of which the human mind is capable. From ancient Egypt to Greece and Rome, from West Africa to Siberia, from the Hindu concept of Brahman and the endless cycle of creation to the eternal Dreaming of the Australian Aboriginals, the same themes recur, as humankind engages with the great mysteries of life and death.

Many mythologies start before the dawn of time, with the coming into consciousness of a creator god, such as the Egyptian Re. Re himself is described as the awareness of an all-encompassing divine being, Nebertcher, the lord without limit. Mythological time, unlike clock time, is cyclical rather than linear. It presupposes what the writer Mircea Eliade called "the myth of the eternal return." It is set in motion by a particular event—in Egypt, the call of the Benu bird as it alighted upon the first land. It will come to an end eventually, and the cycle of creation will begin again. The mythology of the Aztec and Maya, and of Native American nations such as the Navajo, describes this world as being the fifth one. For the Navajo, the first four worlds were beneath this one, from which humanity climbed up in the myth of the emergence. For the Aztec, four suns had shone on previous creations before this, the world of the sun Nahui Ollin, which is blown across the sky by the breath of the god Quetzalcoatl.

The Maya believed that this current cycle of creation began on August 13, 3114 BC. Although they projected events forward until at least 4772 CE, they did not think it would continue forever. Their sacred book, the *Chilam Balam*, tells us: "All moons, all years, all days, all winds, reach their completion and pass away. So does all blood reach its place of quiet, as it reaches its power and its throne. Measured was the time in which they could praise the splendour of the Trinity. Measured was the time in which they could know the sun's benevolence. Measured was the time in which the grid of the stars would look down upon them; and through it, keeping watch over their safety, the gods trapped within the stars would contemplate them." Even the dualistic philosophy of Zoroastrianism, with its opposing gods of good and evil, Ahura Mazda and Ahriman, was set in motion when the god of eternal time, Zurvan, gave birth to the twin gods.

One thing that all mythologies agree on is that the world was created by the deliberate act of a divine being, and that men and women were created especially to live in it. In the Mandan creation myth, First Creator and Lone Man send a mud hen down to fetch sand from the bottom of the primeval flood, in order to make the land. The Ainu of Japan tell how the creator Kamui sent a water wagtail down from heaven to accomplish the same task. According to the Yoruba people in West Africa, the world was made when Obatala, the son of the great sky god Olorun, threw earth from a snail shell, and got a pigeon and a hen to scatter it. The supreme gods of Africa tend, like Olorun, to withdraw from their creation leaving the main work to their successors. In the original myth preserved by the priests of the Fon sky cult, it is the androgynous deity

Creator gods tend to be male, but much of the work of creation may be delegated to a goddess. For example, among the Keres of the American Southwest, Utsiti, the creator god, who made the world from a clot of his own blood, sent his daughter Iatiku with her sister to make the earth fruitful. Iatiku sends her son to lead the people up into this world, and then Iatiku and her sister sing a creation song, all the while casting seeds and images of their song out of a basket given them by Spider Woman.

We still talk of "mother earth." Native Americans consider this as a fact. Smohalla, the Wanapam founder of the Dreamer religion in the mid-19th century, said: "You ask me to plow the ground! Shall I take a knife and tear my mother's bosom? Then when I die she will not take me to her bosom to rest. You ask me to dig for stone! Shall I dig under her skin for her bones? Then when I die I cannot enter her body to be born again. You ask me to cut grass and make hay and sell it, and be rich like white men! But how dare I cut off my mother's hair?" An Anglo-Saxon charm beseeches the favor of "Erce, Erce, Erce, Mother of Earth" with similar fervor. Yet, despite the obvious connection between agricultural and human fertility, the earth is not always female. The Egyptians, for example, worshiped Geb as god of the earth, and his sister-bride Nut as the goddess of the sky.

The first human images known to us are the so-called Venuses found in Upper Paleolithic remains (35,000–10,000 B.C.). From the way these statues are positioned and located in cave hearths, niches, and graves, they are interpreted as cult images—the Mother Guardians of the daily life, death, and rebirth of the people. These statues appear in Europe with the appearance of the Cro-Magnons. But much earlier, during the Neanderthal period (dating from at least 200,000 B.C.), evidence shows that great magical power was attributed to the earth as Mother of Life and Death. Neanderthals buried their dead curled in fetal position, painted red; bones were painted with red ochre. Analogically, the dead were to reenter the earth (the tomb, the womb) to be reborn again. A Neanderthal corpse found in Shanidar Cave in northern Iraq had been laid to rest on pine boughs and strewn with wild flowers. Even earlier than this, a remarkable find at La Ferrassie, in the French limestone country, shows the beautiful resonance that was felt in the minds and hearts of these earliest people between life, death, and the Mother.

The earth was seen by all primal people as the source of nourishment, protection, power, and the mystery of cyclic recurrence. Perhaps the first human analogy made was between the earth and the female, who performed the same functions on an individual level. Especially awesome was the woman's ability to bleed rhythmically with the moon's phases, and her periodic swelling up and dramatic expulsion of a new being. Paintings of the mother giving birth, with the expulsed child still connected to her via the umbilical cord, are found throughout the Cro-Magnon caves. Childbirth isa powerful drama and ritual. To imagine the enormous impact of pregnancy and childbirth on our human ancestors, we have to remember that Palaeolithic people, like many aboriginal people today, did not know the connection between intercourse and pregnancy; the male role might have been seen as "opening" the womb, but the pregnancy itself was seen as resulting from a magical intercourse between the mother and the spirit world—or it was seen as a parthenogenetic act, the woman as spontaneous and autonomous creator of life.

In these cave drawings of childbirth and in the Venus statues, as well as in many images of gravid animals, the fertility of earth and woman was imaged and celebrated as a spiritual-magical act, to ensure the year's abundance of game and fruit. The seasonal return of vegetation and young animal life following winter and apparent death gave early humans the idea of a magical-cyclical rebirth of their own kind. Entombments—whether cave graves or the later underground vaults and collective burial mounds—were ways of returning bodies to the womb of Mother Earth, where they waited for rebirth. According to Barbara Mor:

> *"In the world's oldest creation myths, the female god creates the world out of her own body. The Great Mother everywhere was the active and*

> *autonomous creatrix of the world and, unlike the aloof and self-righteous patriarchal gods who only recently usurped her mountain-throne, the ancient Goddess was always there—alive, immanent—within her creation; no ontological scapegoater, she was wholly responsible for both the pain and the good of life. (38)*"

Nowhere has worship of the eternal female been so strong as in India, where various goddesses are worshiped under the enveloping spell of Mahadevi, the great goddess. Devi is the consort of the god Shiva, and is worshiped as benign Parvati or Uma or as ferocious and vengeful Durga or Kali. Sankara wrote of her in the 9th century, "Your hands hold delight and pain. The shadow of death and the elixir of immortal life are yours." The combination of "delight and pain" is not confined to India. The great goddess of ancient Mesopotamia, variously called Ishtar and Inanna, also combined the roles of goddess of love and goddess of war. These dual aspects are explored in the Epic of Gilgamesh, in which she first desires Gilgamesh and then, when he rejects her, exacts a terrible revenge. The Egyptian Isis became absorbed into Roman myth, and it is she who speaks, with the unmistakable voice of the great goddess, to Lucius, the hero of Apuleius' novel *The Golden Ass*, when he is initiated into her cult: "I am Nature, the universal Mother, mistress of all the elements, primordial child of time, sovereign of all things spiritual, queen of the dead, queen also of the immortals, the single manifestation of all gods and goddesses that are."

In the Mysteries of Eleusis in ancient Greece, the great goddess formed the central focus of Greek religion.

These rituals, open only to the initiated, related to the myth of the grain goddess Demeter, and her daughter Persephone, the ineffable maiden. Those who witnessed the rites were assured of a new birth in death. The Mysteries were thought by the Greeks to "hold the entire human race together." Such a belief illustrates the crucial importance of myth in holding the world together, just as the cosmic serpent coils securely around the earth in the Fon creation story. Australian Aborginal stories about the Dreamtime, such as the Gunwinggu story of Lumaluma, are not just entertainments or nursery tales—they are sacred charters for existence.

The ceremonies, rituals and myths originating out of the sacred cults of the Great Mother frequently rested on the intimate relationship between the human communities and the non-human nature. Environment and the land was considered to be an embodiment of the Great Mother who nurtured all life forms. David Leeming and Christopher Fee recount the origins of the worship of the Great Mother Goddess and its close association with the land and fertility:

> "*For time out of mind, an ancient goddess reigned supreme, and the fertile soil of the land beneath her feet bespoke her immeasurable fecundity. Long ages she ruled, and many were her worshippers. Then, 5,000 years ago or more, perhaps in the region where steppe meets sea in the great central land mass where Asia and Europe conjoin, tribes began to shift and migrate, and their movements were to transform this goddess forever. These peoples began to move south and east into the Indian subcontinent,*

> *down into what is now Iran, up to the Baltic, west along the European coast of the Mediterranean to the Atlantic, and even across the ocean to lands past the horizon. Over thousands of years and miles, these people we often call Indo-Europeans divided into many groups and settled in many regions, and ever the goddess travelled with them; always she transformed to suit her people, her face ever reflecting the needs and desires of her children. The demands of her peoples could be harsh, however, and thus over time this goddess – so often beautiful with the love of her followers – could be seen to be terribly transformed, and love sometimes turned to fear among many of her worshippers. The face of the Earth Mother – comely and resplendent with the abundance of her life-giving womb – alternated with a grimmer guise, her maternal, loving laughter at times replaced with the gruesome grimace of a skull's head. (7)*"

The representation of the Great Mother as the nurturer of life as well as a destroyer can be understood in the context of nature. The early communities who initiated the cults of the Great Mother understood the role of nature as a force that sustained life as well as destroyed it. The benevolent Great Mother bestowed life and fertility through crops and at the same time, inspired awe and terror among the human communities through diseases and natural cataclysms.

A large number of terracotta figures, dating from at least 3000 BCE and representing a female deity, have been found in the Indus Valley. These figures – which may remind us of the very famous and much earlier Palaeolithic 'Venuses' found at archaeological sites at Laussel in France and Willendorf in Austria – have led scholars to suggest that a mother goddess cult existed in the Indus Valley long before any possible arrival of Indo-Europeans in the subcontinent. There have been numerous theories surrounding this goddess. Perhaps the most widely accepted is that she is the earliest manifestation of what would become the great Indian goddess Devi, in her many forms. For devotees of Shaktism, for whom Devi or Shakti is the Absolute and the primary focus of devotion, the Indus Valley goddess was the first known manifestation, the first embodiment of the creative energy. "A terracotta image of particular interest to mythologists is one found in the ruins of the Indus Valley city of Mohenjo-daro of the goddess flanked by tigers. The association of the goddess with these powerful animals is reminiscent of the Great Goddess figurine from the Neolithic Çatalhöyük in Anatolia, who is also flanked by images of powerful feline figures (lions or tigers), or the goddess of Minoan Crete, who holds a snake in either hand" (Fee and Leeming 16). These goddesses all suggest power and even terror, as well as the nurturing that emerges naturally from the association of the female figure with birth and creation.

The Vedic goddesses are those whose identities are revealed in the religioustexts. These include Prithvi, Prakriti, Ushas, Vac or Sarasvati, and Aditi. The personification of Earth, Prithvi or Mata Prithvi (Mother Earth), or Dhra (Container of All Things), is a goddess with four arms and green skin. Her consort is Dyaus Pita (Father Sky), and she is said to be the mother of the Goddess of Dawn, Ushas. Prithvi is an early representation of the great Earth Goddess that we discover, for instance, in the Greek Gaia. Although Dyaus would essentially die out in later Hindu mythology, Prithvi remains. One myth tells how her womb became so full that she had to beg the creator for relief. In response, the creator made a beautiful woman, Death, whose tears became diseases and eased Prithvi's burden by destroying her offspring. The Prithvi myth, then, reflects the sense that the goddess, even as the manifestation of Life incarnate, is inevitably balanced by the reality of Death.According to Nanditha Krishna:

> "*In Vedic literature, all of nature was, in some way, divine, part of an indivisible life force uniting the world of humans, animals and plants. The Vedas are dedicated to a variety of pantheistic deities called devas or the Shining Ones, representing the stars in the firmament and forces beyond human knowledge or control. Chief among them was Indra. Soma was a sacred plant and Agni, the divine fire. There are several solar deities: Surya, Savitr and Aditya, while Ushas was the dawn, a female deity. Vishnu was also a solar deity, symbolized by his three steps across the firmament: the morning and evening sun and the midday orb. Pushan represented agriculture. Dyauspitr was the divine father (the sky, father of the heavens), Prithvi was Mother Earth and Vayu, the wind. The Rivers Sarasvati, Sindhu (Indus) and the latter's tributaries––Shutudri, Parushni, Ashkini, Vitasta and Vipasa or the Sapta Sindhava––were all regarded as sacred. Thus the concept of the*

> *sacred environment was established in the Vedic period itself. (11)*"

What all of these goddesses have in common is their role as 'mothers' of creation – without these beings, nothing that is can be realized. In this sense, Prithvi, Prakriti, Ushas, Vac and Aditi are all the same goddess – prefiguration of the cumulative goddess Devi, whose creative energy activates the potential for existence represented by Dyaus, Purusha, Daksha, Prajapati or Brahma. "Earth is the primordial mother of life; she feeds all creatures out of her substance, and again devours all; she is the common grave. She clasps to her bosom the life she has brought forth, denying to it the unbound freedom of celestial space" (Zimmer 75).

With the rise of agriculture and the domestication of animals as the figure of the Goddess became more clearly defined, and with the growing consciousness of the duality of male and female in the generative process from being the Unmarried Mother personifying the divine principle in maternity she became associated with the Young God as her son or consort. While she remained the dominant figure the cult assumed a twofold aspect in the seasonal drama in which both partners m procreation played their respective roles, until ultimately, after the syncretistic Magna Mater had emerged, it acquired a mystical and theological content in Christendom. Then it was interpreted in terms of the Church as the Mater Ecclesia, and the Virgin Mother of the incarnate Son of God as the Madonna. According to Barbara Mor:

> "*Isis, Mawu-Lisa, Demeter, Gaia, Shakti, Dakinis, Shekhinah, Astarte, Ishtar, Rhea, Freya, Nerthus, Brigid, Danu—call Her what you may—has been with us from the beginning and awaits us now. She is the beauty of the green earth, the life-giving waters, the consuming fire, the radiant moon, and the fiery sun. She is Star Goddess and Spiderwoman; she weaves the luminous web that creates the universe. As earth, the great planetary Spirit-Being, She germinates life within Her dark womb. (15)*"

The same life-shaping force is said to have acquired its fullest realization in Minoan Crete. Here "the Minoan Goddess was depicted in clay and porcelain as the Earth-Mother, the Mountain-Mother, the Mistress of trees and the Lady of wild beasts" (Motz 6). She was the earth in all its aspects, the universal mother goddess, mother of fruits, mother and mistress of animals, and had the king and his palace under her special protection. We would thus find in this culture the first evidence of the infinite variety of forms that belong with the image of the maternal divinity. In Egypt, the great female counterpart of Amen-Ra was Mut, the 'world-mother.' She is usually represented as a woman wearing the united crowns of north and south, and holding the papyrus sceptre. In some pictures she is delineated with wings, and in others the heads of vultures project from her shoulders. Like her husband, she is occasionally adorned with every description of attribute, human and animal, probably to typify her universal nature. Mut, like Amen, swallowed up a great many of the attributes of the female deities of Egypt. She was thus identified with Bast, Nekhebet, and others, chiefly for the reason that because Amen had usurped the attributes of other gods, she, as his wife, must do the same. She is a striking example in mythology of what marriage can do for a goddess. Even Hathor was identified with her, as was Ta-urt and every other goddess who could be regarded as having the attributes of a mother. Her worship centred at Thebes, where her temple was situated a little to the south of the shrine of Amen-Ra. She was styled the (lady of heaven' and 'queen of the gods,' and her hieroglyphic symbol, a vulture, was worn on the crowns of Egypt's queens as typical of their motherhood.

The goddess Prithvi is nearly always associated with the earth, the terrestrial sphere where human beings live. In the Vedic myths, furthermore, she is almost always coupled with Dyaus, the male deity associated with the sky. So interdependent are these two deities in the *Rg-veda* that Prithvi is rarely addressed alone but almost always as part of the dual compound *dyavaprthivi,* sky-earth. Together they are said to kiss the center of the world. They sanctify each other in their complementary relationship (4.56.6). Together they are said to be the universal parents who created the world and the gods. As might be expected, Dyaus is often called father and Prithvi mother.

There is the implication that once upon a time the two were closely joined but were subsequently parted at Varuna's decree. They come together again when Dyaus fertilizes the earth (Prithvi) with rain, although in some cases it is said that together they provide abundant rain; it is not clear to what extent Prithvi should be exclusively associated with the earth alone and not the sky as well.

In addition to her maternal, productive characteristics Prithvi (usually along with Dyaus in the *Rg-veda)* is praised for her supportive nature. She is frequently called firm, she who upholds and supports all things. She encompasses all things , is broad and wide, and is motionless, although elsewhere she is said to move freely. Prithvi, with Dyaus, is often petitioned for wealth, riches, and power, and the waters they produce together are described as fat, full, nourishing, and fertile. They are also petitioned to protect people from danger, to expiate sin, and to bring happiness. Together they represent a wide, firm realm of abundance and safety, a realm pervaded by order *(rta),* which they strengthen and nourish.

The parallel that exists between Prithvi and Dyaus is mirrored in the Greek myths as well. The primal deities Gaia and Uranus embody similar characteristics as Prithvi and Dyaus. Whereas Gaia represents the earth, Uranus embodies the sky. The ancient Greeks had several different theories with regard to the origin of the world, but the generally accepted notion was that before this world came into existence, there was in its place a confused mass of shapeless elements called Chaos. These elements becoming at length consolidated (by what means does not appear), resolved themselves into two widely different substances, the lighter portion of which, soaring on high, formed the sky or firmament, and constituted itself into a vast, overarching vault, which protected the firm and solid mass beneath. Thus, came into being the two first great primeval deities of the Greeks, Uranus and Ge or Gaia.

Uranus, the more refined deity, represented the light and air of heaven, possessing the distinguishing qualities of light, heat, purity, and omnipresence, whilst Gaia, the firm, flat, life-sustaining earth, was worshipped as the great all-nourishing mother. Her many titles refer to her more or less in this character, and she appears to have been universally revered among the Greeks, there being scarcely a city in Greece which did not contain a temple erected in her honour; indeed, Gaia was held in such veneration that her name was always invoked when- ever the gods took a solemn oath, made an emphatic declaration, or implored assistance.

Uranus, the heaven, was believed to have united himself in marriage with Gaia, the earth; and a moment's reflection will show what a truly poetical, and also what a logical idea this was; for, taken in a figurative sense, this union actually does exist. The smiles of heaven produce the flowers of earth, whereas his long-continued frowns exercise so depressing an influence upon his loving partner, that she no longer decks herself in bright and festive robes, but responds with ready sympathy to his melancholy mood.

The Olympian creation myth positions Uranus as the son of the Great Mother Earth. In *The Greek Myths*, Robert Graves writes:

> "*At the beginning of all things Mother Earth emerged from Chaos and bore her son Uranus as she slept. Gazing down fondly at her from the mountains, he showered fertile rain upon her secret clefts, and she bore grass, flowers, and trees, with the beasts and birds proper to each. This same rain made the rivers flow and filled the hollow places with water, so that lakes and seas came into being. (32)*"

Two great families were founded by Gaia (Earth) through her unions with her two self-generated partners, first Uranus (Sky) and then Pontos (Sea). As has already been noted, the family that she founded with Uranus was the nobler of the two, bringing into being all the greatest gods and goddesses, while the family that she founded with Pontos consisted mainly of sea beings and monsters. Of her two partners, moreover, only Uranus can be regarded as having been a true husband of hers, for she is linked to Pontos (who has no myths and is barely personified) for genealogical purposes alone. Uranus and Gaia are in fact the primordial couple in Hesiod's account of the earliest history of the world, even if they are not the first beings of all or the progenitors of all subsequent beings; and the first proper myth in that history is the one that tells how Uranus provoked the dissolution of his marriage and his own downfall by his mistreatment of his wife and children. Important though he may have been at this early stage, Uranus makes no further appearance in myth after the end of his union with Gaia (except in so far as he is said to have delivered prophecies to children of his). There is no evidence that he was ever worshipped or played any part in Greek cult; at most, he might be invoked along with other deities in oaths.

Gaia bore three sets of children to Uranus, first a group of primordial gods who were known as the Titans (properly Titanes in Greek), and then two sets of monsters, the one-eyed Kyklopes and the hundred-armed giants who came to be known as the Hekatoncheires or Hundred-Handers. Uranus hated them all, however, and prevented them from emerging into the light, causing such anguish to Gaia that she finally urged them to take action against him. The youngest of the Titans, Kronos, who was the only one who had the courage to do so, laid an ambush for his father, armed with a sickle that his mother had prepared for the purpose; and he cut off the genitals of Uranus as he approached his wife to make love, so bringing their union to a violent end and making it possible for Gaia to bring their children to the light at last. Kronos hurled the severed genitals into the sea, where sea-foam gathered around them to generate the goddess Aphrodite; and some blood dripped from them on to Gaia, causing her to conceive three further sets of children, the Erinyes, Giants and Meliai. The cultural and religious significance of Gaia has been explained by Michael Grant and John Hazel who write:

> "*She was closely associated with oracles and prophecy. It was she, according to tradition, who founded the oracular shrine of Delphi, originally devoted to her worship. She transferred it to Themis; but Themis surrendered her rights to the Titaness Phoebe, who in turn gave the oracle to Apollo. The earth-snake Python belonged to Gaia, and when Apollo killed it, he had to compensate for the murder by establishing the Pythian Games and by employing the Pythian priestess to oversee his oracle. Gaia supervised oaths, many of which were made in her name; she punished those who broke them and sent the Erinyes (Furies) to avenge her. (226)*"

Subsequently, the evolution of the Great Mother Goddess became manifested through the worship of divinities like Rhea, Demeter, Hera, Artemis and Ceres who were closely associated with the land, fertility and nature.

Rhea, the wife of Cronus, and mother of Zeus and the other great gods of Olympus, personified the earth, and was regarded as the Great Mother and unceasing producer of all plant-life. She was also believed to exercise unbounded sway over the animal creation, more especially over the lion, the noble king of beasts. Rhea is generally represented wearing a crown of turrets or towers and seated on a throne, with lions crouching at her feet She is sometimes depicted sitting in a chariot, drawn by lions. In Rome the Greek Rhea was identified with Ops, the goddess of plenty, the wife of Saturn, who had a variety of appellations. She was called Magna-Mater, Mater-Deorum, Berecjoithia-Idea, and also Dindymene. This latter title she acquired from three high mountains in Phrygia, whence she was brought to Rome as Cybele during the second Punic war, in obedience to an injunction contained in the Sibylline books. She was represented as a matron crowned with towers, seated in a chariot drawn by lions.

Demeter was also revered as the great Earth-goddess, patroness of fertility and goddess of the Eleusinian Mysteries; one of the twelve major Olympian gods and one of the six children of Cronos and Rhea. By Zeus (her brother) she was mother of Persephone or Proserpina, with whom she possessed a close association in Greek cult. Her name means 'Mother Earth'. The Romans identified her with the Italian grain-goddess Ceres; she was also identified in ancient times with the Egyptian Isis, and with the Phrygian Cybele, and with her own mother Rhea. Demeter was considered to spend little time on Olympus, preferring instead to live on earth, especially at Eleusis in Attica where the Mysteries she founded commemorated her success in winning the return of her daughter Persephone. They were celebrated annually in autumn, when the drama of the loss and rediscovery of Persephone was re-enacted by the initiates with music and dancing. E.M. Berens explains:

> "*It is necessary to keep clearly in view the distinctive difference between the three Great Earth Goddesses Gaia, Rhea and Demeter. Gaia represents the earth as a whole, with its mighty subterranean forces; Rhea is that productive power which causes vegetation to spring forth, thus sustaining men and animals; Demeter, by presiding over agriculture, directs and utilizes Rhea's productive powers. But in later times when Rhea like other ancient divinities loses her importance as a ruling deity, Demeter assumes all her functions as and attributes, and then becomes the goddess of the life-producing and life-maintaining earth crust. We must bear in mind the fact that man in his primitive state knew neither how to sow, nor how to till the ground; when, therefore he had exhausted the pastures which surrounded him he was compelled to seek another, settled habitations and consequently civilizing influences, were impossible. Demeter, however, by introducing a knowledge of agriculture, put an end, at once and for ever, to that nomadic life which was now no longer necessary. (40)*"

The worship of the female earth divinity has many important facets, whether or not she assumes the dominant role in the partnership with her male consort.

But whatever her name and however varied her worship, she is significant in all periods, either maintaining her own identity or lurking behind, influencing, and colouring more complex and sophisticated concepts of female deity. Gaia, Themis, Cybele, Rhea, Hera, Demeter, and Aphrodite are all, either wholly or in part, divinities of fertility. Certainly, the emotional, philosophical, religious, and intellectual range of the worship of the mother-goddess is vast. It may run the gamut from frenzied orgiastic celebrations, with the castration of her devoted priests, to a sublime belief in spiritual communion and personal redemption; from a blatant emphasis upon the sexual attributes and potency of the female to an idealized vision of love, motherhood, and virgin birth. The *Homeric Hymn to Earth, Mother of All*, in its invocation of Gaia, gives us the essentials of her primary archetype:

> "*About Earth, I will sing, all-mother, deep-rooted and eldest, who nourishes all that there is in the world: all that go on the divine land, all that sail on the sea and all that fly—these she nourishes from her bountifulness. From you, reverend lady, mortal humans have abundance in children and in crops, and it is up to you to give them their livelihood or take it away. Rich and fortunate are those whom you honor with your kind support. To them all things are bounteous, their fields are laden with produce, their pastures are covered with herds and flocks, and their homes are filled with plenty. These rule with good laws in cities of beautiful women and much happiness and wealth attend them. Their sons glory in exuberant joy*

> *and their daughters, with carefree hearts, play in blossom-laden choruses and dance on the grass over the soft flowers. These are the fortunate whom you honor, holy goddess, bountiful deity.*"

The myth of Demeter and Persephone represents another variation of a fundamental and recurring theme—the death and rebirth of vegetation as a metaphor or allegory for spiritual resurrection. Most of the myths about Demeter relate to the loss of her daughter Persephone. When the girl was still very young, her father Zeus, without consulting Demeter, who would have objected, agreed to Hades' request that Persephone should be his bride. Persephone was plucking flowers in the woods near Henna, in the fertile island of Sicily, one of Demeter's favourite lands. She was accompanied by the girls of the place, her playmates, or else by the daughters of Oceanus. Zeus made a beautiful narcissus grow in a shady, flowery dell. Persephone, at a moment when she was separated from her companions, saw the narcissus and plucked it. Immediately the earth opened up and Hades rode forth in his chariot drawn by dark-blue steeds. He snatched the girl up and at once returned with her to his realm below. Persephone shrieked for her mother but nobody came to help her; and when she reached Hades' realm she still continued to pine and would touch no food.

Demeter, when she learnt her daughter had vanished, started an immediate search. According to one account, she heard Persephone's departing cry. Carrying lighted torches, she roamed the earth for nine days and nights, refusing to eat or drink. She then met Hecate, who lived near the fields of Henna in a cave and knew of the abduction. Hecate led Demeter to Helios, the all-seeing sun god, and asked him to tell her what he had witnessed. He unfolded the whole story, but added that Hades, as brother of Zeus, was a worthy husband for the girl and possessed a fine, ample kingdom.

Demeter was so distraught at the news of the abduction that she immediately cast a blight of drought and famine over the earth and especially over her beloved land of Sicily, which had betrayed its trust by not keeping Persephone safe. Descending from Olympus, she wandered throughout the earth. According to the *Homeric Hymn to Demeter*, the goddess wandered across the earth in human form, granting the benefits of agriculture to those who received her kindly, but punishing the inhospitable.

A temple was constructed in her honour at Eleusis and the Eleusinian mysteries were initiated by Celeus. Demeter spent a whole year in the new temple, refusing the company of the gods. Meanwhile the earth was becoming barren, and Zeus realised that if nothing were done to appease his sister, the race of men would soon die out and gods would cease to receive their sacrifices. In an attempt, therefore, to conciliate Demeter, he sent Iris to Eleusis to beg her to rejoin the Olympian gathering. But she refused to listen, unless Persephone were restored to her. So Zeus consented, but with a single condition: Persephone must eat nothing during her stay in the Underworld, for whoever eats and drinks in Hades' kingdom is his forever. Zeus then sent Hermes to fetch the girl, and Hades agreed to part with her. But as she left, he gave her a pomegranate. When Persephone reached Eleusis, Demeter asked her if she had eaten anything in the Underworld. At first Persephone denied eating anything, but Ascalaphus declared that he had seen the girl eating pomegranate seeds and she had to admit it: she had eaten a number of the seeds, variously estimated between four and seven. So Zeus decreed that she must spend a third of each year in Hades' kingdom as his wife. While the grain is in the ground, growing and ripening, that is, from the sowing in autumn to the harvest in early summer, Persephone stays with her mother and the earth is glad. But while the seed-corn is stored away in jars, in the hot summer months, the goddess goes to dwell with her gloomy husband and the earth is parched and barren.

Demeter's name may mean "earth-mother," but her myth and that of Persephone introduce a startling and drastic variation of this eternal and universal archetype. The myth's sexual blatancy is replaced by a more refined and purer concept of motherhood and the love between a mother and daughter. In this guise, with nobility and humanity, the mother-goddess and matriarchy sustained their dominance in the ancient world. Details of the myth continually challenge the patriarchal power of Zeus. The abduction of Persephone ordained by the supreme god so that Hades may have a wife and the Underworld may have a queen is depicted not as a divine right but a brutal rape, seen from the point of view of Demeter, who will not accept the status quo and is mighty enough to modify it. Through compromise, both the will of Zeus and the will of Demeter are fulfilled. Demeter shares the love and the person of her daughter with Hades; Hades has his wife; and Persephone attains honour as queen of the Underworld: the mystic cycle of death and rebirth is explained by a myth accommodating a specific matriarchal religious ritual, promising joy in this life and the next. The Eleusinian mysteries were an inspiring spiritual force and became the one universal mystery religion of the ancient world before Christianity. Indeed, matriarchy was very much alive and well in the patriarchal world of the Greeks and the Romans.

The Great Goddess was the Mother of Wild Animals. The inner recesses and womb-walls of the caverns were alive with magic pictures of her beasts. She was herself an animal, all the animals; in many of the early images she wears an animal mask. As in ancient Chinese Taoism, so in Western pagan religions, the female principle was the transforming animal, the energy of metamorphosis and hence evolution. The brilliant rush of European animal imagery, from Cro-Magnon through Celtic, Nordic, and Teutonic art, and incorporated into medieval bestiaries and illuminated manuscripts, expressed this primal dynamic vision of evolutionary energy as a surge of spirit into multitudinous forms. The Goddess kept her various animal shapes for many thousands of years, among them the doe, the owl, the hare, the vulture, the pig, the cow, the wild mare, the lioness, the crow, the crane, the salmon, the jackal, the hermaphroditic snail, the serpent, the wren, the butterfly and the chrysalis, the spider.

Early human attitude toward animals was totemistic. “Totem” means “related through the mother.” The blood-clan’s solidarity was identified with some specific plant or animal. Through the totem the life of the human group and the ongoing life of nature were made inseparable. This is the meaning of “sacrament”: the absorption by humans of the non-human, or cosmic flow of forms. The secret spirit lives in—and through—the multitude of plant and animal forms which the Goddess can assume at will. This means that any tree or beast, bird or fish or insect, is symbolically/potentially her, and must be related to with magic and respect.

The animism of primal peoples has been called "childish." In fact, it is a profound, experiential perception of the evolutionary relation between all life forms as manifestations of the original *one*—the first cell from which all life multiplied, the original cosmic egg. When human survival depends on such a sensitive rapport with the environment—as it always has, and always will—such a conception is not infantile, but crucial. Human survival does indeed depend on a sacramental relation to nature. Now that this relation has been betrayed, and destroyed, we know how important it was. And is. A sacramental bond between our earliest human ancestors and the natural world was the primary factor in our evolution—not simply as a physical species, but as conscious beings. For this bonding set up a resonance in which all art, all religious ritual, all magical chemic science, all spiritual striving for illumination was born. As primal people have always experienced it, when you look and listen to nature, something appears, something always speaks. Animism is still a valid relationship. If "modern man" neither sees nor hears,

In primitive belief, no animal can be killed against its wish. When a member of a species is struck down, the *one* is wounded. Therefore the hunter must fast and pray to the animal-spirit before the hunt, not simply to ask its pardon but to gain its assent to being killed. The hunted animal is seen to give itself to the hunter, as human food, while its spirit returns to the group form. Because men did all the large-game hunting, and felt themselves to be tracking and slaying brother and sister animals, magic children, like themselves, of Mother Earth—we know they felt guilt, and sought its resolution. After the spilling of blood one must restore harmony with the dead animal, and with the Mother of Animals, as its soul persists through the multiplicity of lives and deaths.

In the Greek mythology and pagan faith, Artemis is the protectress of wildlife. She is one of the twelve great Olympian deities, a goddess of hunting and archery and, paradoxically, a defender of all wild animals, children, and weak things. She was believed to roam the mountains with a band of attendant nymphs and to resent the intrusion of any who would interfere with her or her protégées. In Classical Greek literature she was characterised by a deliberately chosen and forcibly maintained virginity; she punished those who would violate this state, insisted that all her attendants should also be virgins, and defended virginity among mortal men and women. But Artemis was probably not originally a virgin goddess; she seems to derive from an earthmother, whence her association with the many-breasted Goddess of Ephesus. In consequence she was a bringer of fertility and protector of the newly born.

In all accounts, she is a virgin who devotes herself to hunting, and loves wild, untamed lands and their wildlife; hence her title of Agrotera, 'She of the Wild', an epithet already applied to her in Homer. Her favourite hunting-ground is Arcadia, the mountainous heartland of the Peloponnese, and she likes nothing better than to roam through the wilds in the company of her attendant nymphs, who are vowed to virginity like herself. The *Homeric Hymn to Aphrodite* remarks that she never falls under the sway of the goddess of love, 'for archery is her delight, and the slaying of wild beasts in the mountains, and lyres too, and dancing, and piercing cries and shady woods, and' – the poet adds – 'the cities of just men'. The *Odyssey* speaks of her in similar terms, telling how Artemis the archer roams over the mountains of Arcadia, rejoicing in the pursuit of boars and swift deer in the company of her nymphs. A gentler side of her nature is shown in her concern for the young of all living things, whether of wild beasts, as an aspect of her nature as the protectress of wild animals, or of human beings. Robin Hard explains:

> "*Artemis' connection with wild animals connects her, not with any Greek goddess, but with the old deity who is often called the Mistress of Wild Animals, a great goddess of very ancient origin who was honoured under various names by the people of Minoan Crete, pre hellenic Greece and Asia Minor. As we will see, Artemis was equated with two Cretan goddesses of that type, Britomartis and Diktynna. The etymology of her name is too uncertain to provide any evidence on her origin; it seems to appear in Linear B, although this is not entirely certain. We can be sure, however, that she was originally independent of Apollo and Leto. If she originated as a Mistress of the Animals, it must be acknowledged that she has undergone a considerable change, since the Aegean and Eastern goddesses of that type were mature mother goddesses while Artemis is young and virginal (except in her cult at Ephesus, where she was represented as a many-breasted fertility-goddess). (187)*"

The Romans identified Artemis with the Italian woodland goddess Diana, who was not unlike her in many respects. The Italian goddess had no native statues of course, so in art the familiar figure of the huntress Artemis (Diane) was used for both alike. As has been mentioned, the goddess is typically portrayed as a young and beautiful woman, with her chiton girt up to the knee, generally armed with a bow and quiver, and regularly accompanied by a stag or other beast. She is also shown in long robes, however. In so far as she came to be identified with the moon, her head may be surmounted by a crescent. Her emblems, besides attendant beasts and weapons, include the torch, which is a common attribute of goddesses of fertility because light is very commonly associated with life and birth.

Across multiple cultures, the position of the Mother Goddess has often been invariably linked to the sacredness and fertility of the earth. As the Mother Goddess, Nature/Earth is a sustaining force who nurtures all life forms. Thus, the reverence for the earth was born out of the cults worshipping the Mother Goddess, a personification of the earth or nature.

CHAPTER FOUR

TOTEMISM AND ANIMISM

Nature and society are closely interrelated across several native and indigenous cultures of Africa and America. Dubbed primitive and savage by the colonisers, these native cultures had sustained a profound and intimate relationship with the ecology and non-human nature through their myths and religious practices.

When the first European explorers arrived on the North American continent in the late 15th century, they did not find an empty land. More than 2 million Native Americans representing at least 1,000 different tribes were living in North America. Native Americans inhabited regions ranging from the frozen Arctic to subtropical Florida, from the Pacific Ocean to the Atlantic. They lived on the tundra, in the mountains and woodlands, on the plains and prairies, in the swamps of the Southeast and the deserts of the Southwest. Far from being the single culture labelled "Indians" by Europeans, Native Americans represented a multitude of highly developed cultures and spoke hundreds of different languages.

Wherever they lived, Native Americans of North America developed lifestyles, worldviews, religions, traditions, and mythologies as varied as the environments they inhabited. In the Arctic, where people depended on the creatures of the sea for sustenance, myths identified the powerful beings that controlled the supply of these animals, who needed to be honoured and obeyed. Along the Northwest Coast, people who fished for salmon developed a mythology in which salmon played a primary role. In the Southwest, where a corn-based agriculture predominated, legends about corn were prominent. Groups whose lives depended on hunting told stories about the origin, loss, and recovery of game animals. The climate, the weather, the geography, the sources of food, and the people's way of life all influenced the legends people told.

In the history of a people lie the roots of the people's culture, religion, traditions, rituals, and mythology. Little, however, is known about the early history of Native Americans. Native Americans were not native to the North American continent. Fossil remains of dinosaurs dating back millions of years have been found in North America. However, no fossil evidence has been found of human presence in North America earlier than about 38,000 years ago. Details about the first Americans' arrival are lost in prehistory. Through various scientific methods, however, a picture has begun to develop. Radiocarbon dating of artifacts and sites where animals were killed, DNA studies comparing Native Americans to other population groups, and studies by linguists of similarities and differences among Native American languages have led scientists to conclude that the first humans in North America began arriving from Asia about 40,000 to 35,000 years ago.

Between 10,000 and 8000 BC, the Ice Age ended with the final retreat of the northern glaciers. During this time, the big-game species that had been the primary prey of Paleo-Indian hunters became extinct. As the climate warmed, new animal and plant species filled in the gaps left by those that died out. The Clovis and other spear-point cultures began to give way to regional variants generally called Archaic cultures, which flourished from about 5000 to 1000 b.c. The Archaic, or Foraging, Period was characterized by migratory hunting, trapping of small game, fishing, and gathering of edible wild plants. As animal prey became scarcer, people became more dependent on plant foods. The cultivation of crops such as squash, beans, and maize (corn) was introduced. In some parts of the continent, people began to settle in permanent villages. During this period, people of the Southeast began making pottery. The practice gradually spread throughout North America.

The change from a nomadic, hunting and gathering culture to a more sedentary, agriculture-based culture was the beginning of what is called the Formative Period. In addition to the establishment of villages and the development of agriculture, the Formative Period was characterized by pottery making, weaving, and trade.

Across the continent, cultures became more diverse. Ceremonies and ritual gained increasing importance in people's lives, and carvings in stone expressed people's beliefs. As the people's way of life changed from hunting to agriculture, it is likely that their myths changed as well. The mythology of hunting societies is dominated by tales about the game animals so important to life. Myths of agricultural societies focus more on the fertility of crops and rainmaking.

In the Southeast, the Ohio River valley, and along the Mississippi River and its tributaries, unique mound-building cultures arose beginning around 1800 BC. These cultures were characterized by the construction of huge earthworks, some in geometric shapes and others—called effigy mounds—in the form of animals and birds. These structures and the ornaments, pottery, carved figures, and other artifacts found in mounds hint at the wealth of myth and legend of the mound builders, which unfortunately have not survived to the present day.

For the many different Native American peoples, everything changed following contact with Europeans after Columbus landed in the Americas in 1492. European contact added new dimensions to old mythologies, and new traditions developed. For instance, the introduction of the horse by Spanish conquistadores in the 1600s radically changed the culture of the Plains tribes. The oral tradition of the Plains people celebrates the coming of the horse, although it does not attribute its origin to the Spaniards. These animals were too important a gift to have come in such an ordinary way. Many tribes told stories of how a vision seeker acquired horses through supernatural encounters. Of course, the changes that prompted the development of other new Native American myths were far from beneficial. The near-extinction of the buffalo caused by European hunters in the 1800s was devastating for the Plains tribes. The loss of the buffalo figures in numerous legends. Displacement and resettlement of tribes had an equally devastating effect. Cultures and traditions were altered or destroyed, native languages died out, and countless Native Americans died from European diseases, warfare, and genocide.

America was not the only continent whose native and indigenous culture and religious traditions were threatened by colonial settlers. Africa was another continent that bore the brunt of colonialism and its indigenous tribes struggled to preserve their myths, languages and religious practices.

The first impression one gets of Africa is its size. Africa is the world's second largest continent in area (after Asia). The continent spans about 5,000 miles from north to south and about 4,600 miles from east to west at its widest part in the north. The geography of Africa is as varied as one might expect in such an immense area. Strips of fertile land at northern and southern extremes of the continent gradually fade into the vast reaches of the Sahara Desert in the north and the smaller Kalahari Desert in the south. Narrow bands of brush and scrub forest and grasslands border the deserts. Tall mountains—many of which are extinct volcanoes—tower over the rolling, grassy savannas. Broad and powerful rivers cut across the continent, making their way to the sea. In the center of Africa is a great equatorial rain forest. Wherever the land was capable of supporting human life, people settled. They developed agriculture and animal husbandry, learned metalworking, founded cities, and built empires.

To refer to "Africans" or "African culture" as if the inhabitants of this enormous continent represent one people is an error. People's ways of life, religions, traditions, and mythologies vary greatly from region to region and even from one tribe to a neighbouring tribe.

Wherever they lived, Africans developed lifestyles, worldviews, religions, traditions, and mythologies that were as different from one another as their physical environments.

Also because of its size, outside influences on Africa varied from place to place. The great civilization of ancient Egypt dominated other cultures that developed along the Nile River. Peoples on the Red Sea coast were influenced by the peoples of southern Arabia across the sea. North Africa, which borders the Mediterranean Sea, is just eight miles across the Strait of Gibraltar from Europe. It was settled by the ancient Phoenicians, Greeks, Romans, and Arabs, all of whom exerted their own influences on North African culture, traditions, and mythologies. Central Africa, south of the Sahara, remained uninfluenced by outside civilizations for millennia. Its peoples developed their own unique religions, worldviews, and mythologies.

Africa has a long and dynamic history that goes back millions of years. Human life began in Africa. Anthropological evidence in the form of fossil skulls, bone fragments, and other artifacts shows that the first hominids—upright primates who walked on two legs—evolved in East Africa around 5 million years ago. By 700,000 years ago, hominids who migrated out of Africa had spread throughout Asia and Europe. Fossil remains of the first modern humans—Homo sapiens—that date back 160,000 years were found in Ethiopia in 2003. This is evidence that modern humans also evolved in Africa and spread out from there.

Over many thousands of years, the geography of Africa has changed more than once. Between around 5500 and 2500 BC., the continent's climate became wetter. The northern half of Africa became a lush prairie, populated by hunters, herders, and farmers. Archaeologists have learned about these people's lives from the thousands of rock paintings discovered throughout the region. Scenes showing everyday activities, rituals, musicians, and decoratively costumed dancers give a glimpse into the customs, traditions, and ceremonial lives of these ancient people. Nothing, however, is known about their myths.

About 4,000 years ago the climate changed again; it became increasingly drier. Lands that were once fertile became desert. Today, the sands of the Sahara cover the beds of ancient rivers and the ruins of cities that flourished long ago. The people of the Sahara migrated to more hospitable lands. They took with them their religions, customs, traditions, and mythology. From the Sahara, people dispersed in three directions. Some went north to the coast of the Mediterranean Sea. There, they merged with the local people and formed the Berber culture. Some settled in the fertile lands along the Nile River and later became known as Libyans. Still others migrated south into the heart of the continent.

Historically, West Africa is associated with the slave trade, which existed before the coming of Europeans. From the mid-15th century on, Europeans played an increasingly prominent role in the trade, which grew significantly as a result. Some historians estimate that between 1450 and 1850, some 28 million Africans were forcibly removed from central and western Africa. These men and women were sent to European colonies and plantations in the Americas and the Caribbean as slaves. Displaced Africans brought their rich cultural traditions, religions, oral arts, and mythologies with them. Vodun, the religion of the Fon of Benin, is still practiced in Cuba, Haiti, and parts of the United States. African folktales about trickster animals such as the tortoise, hare, and spider assumed new lives in American folk tales. Stories about Br'er Rabbit that originated in the American South and became popular throughout the United States in the 1800s derived from the Bantu trickster hare, Kadimba.

Although details of Native American myths vary from culture to culture, certain themes are universal. Throughout North America there are creation accounts—legends about the origins of the universe, Earth, heavenly bodies, human beings, animals, and important plants. For almost all tribes—except for those in the arid Southwest—in the beginning the world was covered with primordial waters before land was created. Myths abound about diving animals and birds that bring up mud from the bottom of the waters to make the Earth. In tales from the Southwest, four or five worlds of different colors or elements are stacked atop each other, and people ascend from one dying world to the next until they reach the last, present world. Universally, myths express a reverence for nature and an understanding of the need to honor the animals that gave their lives to sustain human life. Many myths center on instructions about the appropriate ways to approach, take the life of, and thank game animals.

Every culture has its tales of culture heroes who brought the gift of the essentials of life, such as light, fire, rain, game animals, and sacred plants. Culture heroines also exist—women associated with fertility, conception, pregnancy, birth, agriculture, and skills such as pottery, weaving, and basket making. Every culture also has its tales of tricksters—beings so clever they often outwitted even themselves— who were also often seen as culture heroes. warrior twins are a variant of culture heroes found in many different traditions. Regional variations reflect specific cultures. However, the twins' births are typically shrouded in mystery. They are frequently sons of the Sun, attain adulthood rapidly, have supernatural powers, and are capable of feats of magic. Typically, the twins enter on a quest to their father in order to obtain weapons and lore, having many adventures, undergoing ordeals and tests, and slaying monsters in the process. They return to their people triumphant and share the knowledge they have gained—thus assuring the perpetuation of ritual knowledge and traditions.

Along with the origins of life, the origins of death and the nature of the after-world also play a role in the mythologies of almost every culture. Concepts of life after death vary widely. The Natchez sent their rulers into the afterlife accompanied not only by a wealth of treasures but also by women and servants who had been slain in order to attend them in the next world. For some tribes, the souls of the dead lived on in the spirit world in much the same way they lived on Earth—hunting, tending crops, gathering foods, and fishing.

Africa did not develop one overall myth system, because Africa itself does not have one people, one history, or one language. African peoples speak more than 2,000 different languages. They have almost as many traditions of behaviour and belief and mythologies. Still, common themes do exist. Linguists divide indigenous African languages into four distinct language families: Afro-Asiatic, Nilo- Saharan, Niger-Congo, and Khoisan. A fifth group includes Indo-European languages (Afrikaans, English, and Creole Portuguese) and Malayo-

Polynesian.

Egypt and the Nile kingdoms of Nubia and Kush had long traditions of writing. It is from written records that we know about their deities, traditions, and mythologies. Similarly, the Meroic empire had a writing system acquired through its ties to the Semitic peoples of southern Arabia. The most important factor in the spread of literacy throughout Africa was the Islamic invasions, which began with the conquest of Egypt in AD 646. By the 1300s the kingdoms of the Sahel had been converted to Islam and became centers of Islamic learning. At first, many Africans dealt with two languages—their native languages and Arabic. Eventually, though, they began to write in their own languages using the Arabic alphabet. With literacy, Africans could record their own histories, legends, and myths. An early known example of East African literature, dated 1520 and written in Arabic, is a history of the city-state of Kilway Kisiwani. Histories of other city-states written in Swahili appeared soon after. The earliest known work of literature—a Swahili epic poem titled *Story of Tambuka*—was written in 1728.

Africa has a long and rich oral tradition that survives to this day. Cultural beliefs, traditions, histories, myths, legends, and rules for living have been passed down orally from generation to generation. The keepers of the oral tradition are bards—tribal poet-singers and storytellers. Bards are charged with remembering and passing along a culture's history and tradition through story and song. Almost all existing epics come from recordings of live performances by African bards known by the French term *griot* in western Africa.

African storytelling has always been an interactive process, in which audiences are encouraged to help tell the story. Songs are an important part of the story. Often, a bard will team up with a singer to perform myths and legends. The bard will act as the narrator, introducing the characters and telling their stories. At times, the singer will take over and lead the audience in what is known as a "call and response" style of storytelling. Taking the part of one of the characters, the singer will sing a line or two and then encourage the audience to respond with a specific refrain.

Because they are part of an oral tradition, African myths and legends are flexible and creative, depending on who is telling the story and why. Tribal elders may use a particular legend to teach religious beliefs or reinforce proper behaviour, while children often tell the same stories for their own amusement. For example, a storyteller who wants to warn children about the dangers of wandering off may tell a folk tale in which a disobedient child is shredded to bits by a sharp-toothed lion. Choosing the same tale to teach mothers to keep track of their children, the storyteller might create a character of a foolish mother whose laziness is responsible for her child being eaten by the lion. A child who tells the same story to a group of friends might want to emphasize how clever children are, making the disobedient child outsmart the lion by doing something silly, like farting in its face to get away. An adult telling the same story might show the father saving the child from the lion by diverting the lion's attention with a whistle. According to Patricia Ann Lynch and Jeremy Roberts:

> "*present-day religions are an important source of African mythology. The mythologies of*

> *African cultures cannot be separated from African religions. Many African religions are living religions not only in Africa but also in parts of the world where people of African descent live. It is through these contemporary religions that we have learned much about traditions, practices, and beliefs of the past. (xvi-xvii)*"

The native American, following the pace of "Indian time," still lives connected to the nurturing womb of mythology. Mysterious but real power dwells in nature—in mountains, rivers, rocks, even pebbles. White people may consider them inanimate objects, but to the Indian, they are enmeshed in the web of the universe, pulsating with life and potent with medicine. As Ernst Cassirer has written, "The mythical world is at a much more fluid and fluctuating stage than our theoretical world ... The world of myth is a dramatical world—a world of actions, of forces, of conflicting powers. In every phenomenon of nature it sees the collision of these powers. Mythical perception is always impregnated with these emotional qualities" (*Essay on Man* 1962).

The world of the Pueblo Indians is bounded mythically and geographically by four sacred mountains, where holy men still go on pilgrimages to pray for rain and to gather medicines. The associations between geography and mythic events are strong; the mountains of the Northwest, for example, were believed by the native inhabitants to have once been people who fought, schemed, loved, and were eventually given the form they now have by the all-powerful One, mostly as punishment for making trouble. The firmament is filled with stars and planets who were once on earth, human lovers fated to chase each other across the evening sky into eternity. Such roles are not fixed, either; the sun, moon, and morning star seem free to take human form and roam the earth, seeking love and other adventures.

To those used to the patterns of European fairy tales and folktales, Indian legends often seem chaotic, inconsistent, or incomplete. Plots seem to travel at their own speed, defying convention and at times doing away completely with recognizable beginnings and endings. Coyote is a powerful creator one moment, a snivelling coward the next. Infants display alarming talents or powers; births and deaths alternate as fast as night and day. To try to apply conventional (Western) logic is not only impossible but unnecessary; spinning out a single image or episode may be the salient feature of—indeed, the whole reason for—telling a tale, and stories are often told in chains, one word, character, or idea bringing to mind a related one, prompting another storyteller to offer a contribution. The howling wind, the bubbling brook, the shrieking magpie all suggest, in their vital immediacy, stories, out of which legends are created. Stories are told for adults and children alike, as elements in solemn ceremonies and as spontaneous creations. Rather than being self-contained units, they are often incomplete episodes in a progression that goes back deep into a tribe's traditions.

Legends, of course, vary according to a people's way of life, the geography and the climate in which they live, the food they eat and the way they obtain it. The nomadic buffalo hunters of the Plains tell stories very different from those of Eastern forest dwellers. To the Southwestern planters and harvesters, the coming of corn and the changing of seasons are of primal concern, while people of the Northwest who make their living from the sea fill their tales with ocean monsters, swift harpooners, and powerful boatbuilders. All tribes have spun narratives as well for the features of their landscape: how this river came to be, when these mountains were formed, how our coastline was carved.

Legends as well as cultures overlap and influence each other, not only when people of different tribes live in adjacent territory, but even when they encounter each other through migration or trade over long distances. Excavations of a pre-Columbian Hohokam site in Arizona uncovered a Mayan-style ball court, a hard rubber ball, copper bells, and exotic parrot feathers, all of which had to have come from central Mexico, more than a thousand miles away. An Aztec-like image of the male face of the sun, surrounded by rays, is found painted and chipped into rock walls of the Southwestern United States as well as in contemporary Pueblo art. Nao'tsiti, the lost White Sister, and Bahana, the White Brother of Hopi prophecy, may embody memories of the Mayan Kukulcan or the Aztec Quetzalcoatl, the white Plumed Serpent god who comes from the east across the Great Water. Images and tokens were carried to faraway peoples along with trade goods; white seashells and abalone shells are mentioned several times in ancient myths as ritual objects in areas five hundred to a thousand miles from the Pacific Coast.

Yet with all their regional images and variations, a common theme binds these tales together—a universal concern with fundamental issues about the world in which humans live. We encounter again and again, in a fantastic spectrum of forms, North and South, East and West, the story of the children of the sun, of the twin brothers who bring culture, of the sacred four directions, of worlds piled on top of each other, of primordial waters, of perpetual destruction and re-creation, of powerful heroes and tricksters—Veeho, Rabbit, Coyote, and Spider Man.

History enters the mythic world obliquely, but leaves its definite mark in characters and incidents. Many tales and cycles embody the collective experience of a particular tribe, perhaps compacting into a single dramatic myth migrations, natural disasters, and other major events that occurred over generations and centuries, with mythically transformed references to "historical" episodes—the creation and fall from power of the Iroquois League; first sightings and later encounters with Europeans and other whites, beginning with missionaries and traders, later with armed soldiers; the suppression of religion by the Spanish and the Pueblo uprisings of 1680; the arrival in and displacement from traditional homelands and the accompanying deaths or devastations; the dramatic watershed encounters at Fort Stanwix and at Rosebud, Little Bighorn, and Wounded Knee. By moving often cataclysmic events into the realm of myth or folklore, the storyteller can at once celebrate, mourn, and honour the past—and look ahead to a time when the great heroes may return to their people, bearing powerful medicine to restore former glory.

But these legends do not merely confront cosmic questions about the world as a whole. They are also magic lenses through which we can glimpse social orders and daily life: how families were organized, how political structures operated, how men caught fish, how religious ceremonies felt to the people who took part, how power was divided between men and women, how food was prepared, how honour in war was celebrated. The images that transmit certain timeless concerns are resonant: in one account of the conflict between the sexes, men and women decide to live in separate camps, divided not only by anger and a brooding sense of injustice, but by a mighty river as well.

The links between the historic past and the present through myth are strong. Archaeologists' evidence shows that the Iroquois of the Northeast have possessed a viable material culture continuously for several thousand years, a chain reflected in an extant body of folklore which has survived despite the attempts of many generations of white society to eradicate (or negatively stereotype) Indian history and culture. The effects of white culture on many other regions, with the notable exceptions of the Southwest and the Plains, and to a degree the Northwest, have been devastating, with whole bodies of Indian literature erased, or warped beyond recognition in their contemporary representations. In the words of Richard Erdoes and Alfonso Ortiz:

> "*Where legends endure, they do so fiercely. Tunka, the stone god, is the Sioux's oldest god, and men still carry oddly shaped pebbles, bits of flint, or lumps of fossil agate in their medicine bundles. They still pray to special sacred rocks and tell legends about them. Rivers, lakes, waterfalls, and mountains are the abodes of spirits and often appear as living characters in stories. Even today a Sioux or Cheyenne might say, "I felt the sacred pipe move in my hands. It was alive. Power flowed from it." Or, "When I touched the sacred sun dance pole, I felt that it was flesh, warm flesh." The ancient tokens and*

symbols still exist and are carefully preserved. Modern equipment is no match. When the Sioux medicine man Lame Deer first traveled on a modern jet, he immediately related his Boeing 707 to the Wakinyan, the Thunderbirds, whose awesome power ignites the lightning. The airplane suffered greatly by comparison. (13)"

Legends as well as cultures overlap and influence each other, not only when people of different tribes live in adjacent territory, but even when they encounter each other through migration or trade over long distances. Excavations of a pre-Columbian Hohokam site in Arizona uncovered a Mayan-style ball court, a hard rubber ball, copper bells, and exotic parrot feathers, all of which had to have come from central Mexico, more than a thousand miles away. An Aztec-like image of the male face of the sun, surrounded by rays, is found painted and chipped into rock walls of the Southwestern United States as well as in contemporary Pueblo art. Nao'tsiti, the lost White Sister, and Bahana, the White Brother of Hopi prophecy, may embody memories of the Mayan Kukulcan or the Aztec Quetzalcoatl, the white Plumed Serpent god who comes from the east across the Great Water. Images and tokens were carried to faraway peoples along with trade goods; white seashells and abalone shells are mentioned several times in ancient myths as ritual objects in areas five hundred to a thousand miles from the Pacific Coast. According to Jon E. Lewis:

"*Although generally bound to the Earth, the Amerindian was especially bound to one corner of it. Common to Amerindian religion was the belief that each nation was created for its own land, and it was special to them. In the words of Geronimo, the famed Apache war chief:*

For each tribe of men Usen [God] created he also made a home. In the land for any particular tribe He placed whatever would be best for the welfare of that tribe, the Apaches and their home [were] each created for the other by Usen himself.

And in the words of Luther Standing Bear, who became chief of the Oglala Sioux in 1905:

The American Indian is of the soil, whether it be the region of forests, plains, pueblos, or mesas. He fits into the landscape, for the hand that fashioned the continent also fashioned the man for his surroundings. He once grew as naturally as the wild flowers; he belongs just as the buffalo belonged.

Just as the Native Americans had no common religion, they had no universal mythology. The multitude of tribes each developed their own stories about the creation of the earth, the coming of the first people, and the lives and doings of deities and heroes. (16)"

African religion dramatizes its unity in the universal appeal to the spirits that animate all of nature. Humans, stones, trees, animals, lakes, rivers, and mountains are conjoined in one grand movement toward the continuation of life. The ideas of reciprocity, circularity, and continuity of the human community are essential elements in the discourse on African religion. At the core of this continuity is the belief that ancestors remain active in the community of the living. Almost all other actions on Earth are dependent on the eternal community that encompasses the unborn, the living, and the deceased.

Fractured by numerous cultural and spiritual intrusions, African religion has withstood the worst of human brutality and cruelty against other humans with solemn resilience. There are some beliefs and aspects of life and knowledge that are consistent across the continent. For example, human beings originated on the continent of Africa, and the earliest human consciousness toward the awesomeness of nature and the mysteries of life and death was an African experience. In Africa, the world exists as a place full of energy, dynamism, and life, and the holding back of chaos by harmonizing the spirit world is the principal task of the human being in keeping with nature. In the African world, spirits exist. This is not a debatable issue in most African societies. The existence of spirits that are employed in the maintenance of balance and harmony represents the continuous search for equilibrium.

The idea that a creator exists is also at the base of this African reality. In fact, African people have lived with the name of a Supreme Deity longer than any other people because the first humans who responded to the unknown with the announcement of awe originated on the African continent. This is not just true in the sense of oral tradition, but in historical time we know that the names of Bes, Ptah, Atum, Ra, Amen, Khnum, Set, Ausar, and Auset are among the oldest names for divinities in the world.

Nothing in ancient African culture was more standard and more consistent than the belief in a First Ancestor. Whether one was in the Nile, Congo, or Niger valley,

Africans accepted the idea of a Supreme Being or a First Ancestor. There is generally the belief that a Supreme Being or First Ancestor arrived with the first ancestor of a group of people in a region. Sometimes these two entities are the same being, and at other times they are separate. An Akan saying is "God is the Great Ancestor." A woman dies and she is remembered for what she did on Earth, and the story is passed down from generation to generation; in the transmission, the story is embellished so that a current generation revels in the supernatural deeds done eons ago. She becomes the First Ancestor. We are in the province of mystery here because the numerous powers that may be called on to explain various phenomena will have their roots in the ancestral world. According to Molefi Kete Asante:

> "*The African Supreme Being, however, rarely plays a role in the daily activities of the people. No one would even think of knowing this being or trying to know him or her as "a personal savior." The Abrahamic deity of Judaism, Christianity, and Islam is quite different from the African God of Yoruba, Zulu, and Gikuyu. Who could fathom the possibilities of the Creator being involved on a personal level with humans? How could one have a personal relationship with God? How could God be a dictator in human life? Thus, the myths, stories, legends, and narratives that are created by the various branches of Popular Traditional African Religion Everywhere (PTARE) are designed to approximate the nature of the God of Gods or, at least, to provide the necessary and attendant assistants in the process of*

maintaining ethics without the universe. (xxiii)"

What is believed intensely all over the continent of Africa is that the Supreme Being, who could be male, female, or both, created the universe, animals, and human beings, but soon retreated from any direct involvement in the affairs of humans. In some cases, in Africa, the Supreme Being does not finish the creation; it is left to other deities to complete. Among the Yoruba, this delegation of creation appears when Olorun, the Owner of the Sky, the Supreme God, starts the creation of the universe and then leaves it to Obatala, a lesser deity, to complete the task. Among the Herero of Namibia, the Supreme God, Omukuru, the Great One, Njambi Kurunga, withdrew into the sky after creating lesser divinities and humans. There are neither temples nor shrines to the God of Gods among most people in Africa. In most cases, the lesser divinities are worshipped, revered, loved, and feared. Asante explains:

> "*Only at the most critical moment when it seems the entire universe is topsy-turvy or the cosmos may fail will the African person appeal to the Creator God. Of course, this situation is not expected. It is probably best summed up by the behavior of the Ewe of southern Ghana, who do not invoke the name of Dzingbe, the Universal Father, unless there is a drought. With a drought comes the possibility that there will be no food, and if there is no food, there will be no life. It is a time of severe crisis. They might then say, "Universal Father, Dzingbe, who rules the sky, to whom we are grateful, mighty is the drought and*

> *we are suffering; let it rain, let the earth be refreshed, let the fields be resurrected and the people prosper!" Otherwise, they do not bother the awesome Dzingbe. (xxiii)*"

Unquestionably, however, the African idea of a creator God who brings justice to the Earth is the most consistent description of the Almighty. Among the Konso of Ethiopia, *Waqa*, the Supreme God, originated morality, social order, justice, and fertility. Waqa gave the breath of life to humans who had been formed, but could neither move nor speak. When Waqa's wife saw the state of humanity, she pleaded with him to do something about human immobility and lack of speech. Waqa then gave humans breath and humans began to speak and to move. Yet when humans die, they must give breath back to Waqa.

The Akan *Nyankopon* had to deal with humans trying to reach God after he had retreated into a distant abode. A woman wanting to reach God had her children stack pounding mortars on each other until they almost reached God. They were one short of reaching God when the woman thought that the only way to succeed was to have one of the mortars taken from the bottom and put on the top to reach God. When this was tried, the whole thing crashed to the Earth. Since that time, no humans have been able to reach the distant abode of God.

The Supreme God stands alone in the African tradition. As the most ancient Africans believed, the aim of humans was to maintain balance, order, and harmony to continue to beat back chaos. One sees this at the beginning of religious history in the relationship of the people of Egypt to their divinities. This is possible because the Supreme God also made possible lesser divinities whose job it was to assist humans in the maintenance of harmony. A Supreme Deity is the progenitor of all other deities. For example, Nyankopon, the truly great Nyame, is personified by the sun in the culture of the Akan, the dynamic center of the state as the sun is of the sky. He is the creator of all gods, and so many golden objects are symbolic of his radiance. The Queen Mother is the daughter of the moon, but only the Supreme Deity is said to be a progenitor of gods.

All natural phenomena might be considered candidates for divinity. The so-called nature divinities appear in many varieties. These are mountains, rivers, and trees that represent certain powerful aspects of the supreme. For example, among the Asante of Ghana, the Tano River and Lake Bosumtwe are seen as divinities. Any natural phenomenon that has been consecrated by certain human achievements, actions, and experiences can become identified with the divine. Thus, the baobab trees that have protected travellers during particular dreadful droughts have become divinities. There are Ohum and Iroko trees, from which special signs have appeared to assist humans moving from one place to another. These, too, have become divinities. All living things have the potential of becoming consecrated as sacred. The gulf that exists between the secular and the sacred in the West does not appear in traditional African religion.

When the waters of the Tano River do not seem to flow as they should, the drummer recites an ancient saying: Pure, pure Tano/If you have gone elsewhere, come/And we shall seek a path for you. Nature gods are more common in West Africa than in Southern Africa.

The western part of the continent is immensely rich in rain forests and rivers. It might be that the people of that region have had to deal with more intense natural phenomena and therefore are more apt to recognize the power of the natural elements. There is, however, among the Zulu of southern Africa, a female deity known as *Inkosazana* who helps corn to grow. Inkosazana, although not strictly a natural deity, does perform like a natural deity because she assists in the harvest, and the community can appeal to her for this assistance. However, Inkosazana is not like a river or mountain that has been deified.

Africans accept that the most common experiences of human beings are with nature. Because nature interacts with humans on a daily basis, it is important to understand how nature figures in daily lives. All nature deities are useful in the recruitment of true believers.

Deities are not inconsequential. They are able to bring about healing or destruction. Sometimes their potency is expressed in charms, medicines, and rites of secret societies. Any force that appears to have magical qualities that are inexplicable must be considered in the realm of the divine. These powers are often like energy, abstract, and invisible; results are visible. They tend to be amoral and forceful, simply manifesting themselves in the Earthly lives of humans.

Indeed, the Earth is a living entity. The Ibo speak of Mother Earth, and the Akan say the Earth is *Asase Yaa*, Mother Earth. Among the Kru of Liberia, the Earth figures in all actions and can keep humans from seeing those who are taken out of the world, those who disappear or who are removed from the land of the living.

Similar themes and beliefs abound in the myths and religious practices of the native Americans. The theme of primeval water covering a not-yet-created earth is perhaps the most prevalent, found in every area except that of the Eskimo, while only the Southwest lacks the episode of a diving creature fashioning the earth from mud. The California regions and the Southwest share tales of the original world parents, Earth and Sky, and the creation of men from rubbings of skin. Among tribes of the Trans-Mississippi West, the determination of the seasons is a prominent theme, and there are many stories across the continent which describe how the four winds came to be. While stories of a creator and of the formation of the universe tend to be more fragmentary, there is clear and universal concern for the beginning of mankind and the foundation of the world in which humans live. An intricate balance and harmony exist between the native American tribes and the natural world. According to David Leeming and Jake Page:

> "*For the traditional Indian, survival depends in part on a delicate balance between the needs and powers of nature's animals and plants and the needs of human beings. A deep harmony within life is established through myths of a dying god or goddess and by rituals in honor of slain animals, the planted and harvested crops, and the sun and rain needed to nourish them. Among other things this harmony requires that people demonstrate self-control and honor the spirit in all things. (60)*"

Birds, animals and objects of nature assume cultural and religious significance in the lives of the native American tribes. Underlying nearly all Native American creation stories is the belief that the people have an intimate connection with everything around them, from trees, to crops, to animals. Regarding the native Americans and their system of beliefs, Jon Lewis writes:

> "*Trees, the winds, the river (which he names 'the Long Person'), all possess life and consciousness in his eyes. The trees moan and rustle, therefore they speak, or are, perchance, the dwelling-place of powerful spirits. The winds are full of words, sighings, warnings, threats, the noises, without doubt, of wandering powers, friendly or unfriendly beings. The water moves, articulates, prophesies, as, for example, did the Peruvian Rimac and Ipurimac – 'the Oracles', 'the Prophesiers'. Even abstract qualities were supposed to possess the attributes of living things. Light and darkness, heat and cold, were regarded as active and alert agencies. The sky was looked upon as the All-Father from whose cooperation with the Mother Earth all living things had sprung. This condition of belief is known as 'animism'. (25)*"

These ritualistic beliefs and mythic origins are ascribed to an ancestor who has been initiated by animal beings into their mysteries, or dances, thus conferring upon him the powers of the initiating creatures; the animals themselves are not regarded as ancestral, nor are the members of the clan akin to the totemic being, except in so far as they possess the powers and practise the rites obtained through the ancestral revelation. The manner of revelation is precisely that in which the Indian everywhere in North America acquires his guardian or tutelary, his personal totem: in fast or trance the man is borne away by the animal-being, taken perhaps to the lodge of its kind, and there given an initiation which he carries back to his people. "The distinctive feature of the North-Western custom, however, is that a totem so acquired may be transmitted by inheritance, so that a man's lineage may be denoted by such a series of crests as appears upon the totem-pole" (Alexander 199). Correspondingly, the number and variety of totemic spirits become reduced, animals or mythic beings of a limited and conventionalized group forming a class fixed by heredity. Yet the individual character of the totem never quite disappears; what is transmitted by birth is the right to initiation into the ancestral mysteries; without this ceremony the individual possesses neither the use of the crest nor knowledge of its myths and songs. Explaining the symbolic significance of the totems, Hartley Burr Alexander writes:

> "*The wooden masks, carved and painted, employed in the initiation ceremonies connected with the clan totems are the ritual representations of the clan myth. Many of these masks are double, the inner and outer faces representing two moods or incidents in the mythic adventure. Frequently the outer is an animal, the inner a human, face — a curious expression of the aboriginal belief in a man-soul underlying the animal exterior. (201)*"

The Indian, brought into contact with the denizens of the forest and prairie, conceived a high opinion of their qualities and instinctive abilities. He observed that they possessed greater cunning in forest-craft than himself, that their hunting instinct was much more sure, that they seldom suffered from lack of provisions, that they were more swift of foot. In short, he considered them to be his superiors in those faculties which he most coveted and admired. Various human attributes and characteristics became personified and even exaggerated in some of his neighbours of wood and plain. The fox was proverbial for craft, the wild cat for stealth, the bear for a wrong-headed stupidity, the owl for a cryptic wisdom, the deer for swiftness. In each of these attributes the several animals to whom they belonged appeared to the savage as more gifted than himself, and so deeply was he influenced by this seeming superiority that if he coveted a certain quality, he would place himself under the protection of the animal or bird which symbolized it. Again, if a tribe or clan possessed any special characteristic, such as fierceness or cunning, it was usually called by its neighbours after the bird or beast which symbolized its character. A tribe would learn its nickname from captives taken in war; or it might even bestow such an appellation upon itself. After the lapse of a few generations the members of a tribe would regard the animal whose qualities they were supposed to possess as their direct ancestor, and would consider that all the members of his species were their blood relations. Jon E. Lewis adds:

> *"A vast and intricate system of tribal law and custom arose from the adoption of totemism. The*

animal from which the tribe took its name might not be killed or eaten, because of its blood-kinship with the clan. Descent from this ancestor postulated kinship between the various members of the tribe, male and female; therefore the female members were not eligible for marriage with the males, who had perforce to seek for wives elsewhere. This often led to the partial adoption of another tribe or family in the vicinity, and of its totem, in order that a suitable exchange of women might be made as occasion required, and thus to the inclusion of two gentes or divisions within the tribe, each with its different totem-name, yet each regarding itself as a division of the tribal family. (27)"

There is a close and intimate relationship between the humans, animals and the environment. As illustrated by the myths, humans and non-human life forms coexist in the natural world. Through the example of the bear myth, Boria Sax illustrates the sacred position held by the animal in the native American culture:

"The Tlingit and many other Indian tribes on the northwest coast of the North American continent have told stories of a young woman who was lost in the woods and was befriended by a bear. At first she was afraid, but the bear was kindly and taught her the ways of the forest. Eventually she became his wife. She grew thick hair and hunted like a bear. When the couple had children, she at first tried to teach them the ways of both bears and human beings. Her human family, however,

would not accept the marriage, and her brothers killed her husband, whereupon she broke completely with the ways of humans. (25)"

The belief in animism- the spiritual idea that all the objects of nature are imbued with souls, was developed by the native tribes over thousands of years living in close association with nature. Depending on nature and ecology for their survival and sustenance, the tribes learnt to respect and revere the various aspects of nature. The Indian tribes understood the vital importance of a power way superior to human agencies- the power of nature that brought about changes in the weather, caused seasonal changes and made the plants grow.

The belief in the power of nature which was integral to native American culture was similarly echoed by the African tribes. A closer study of the myths, culture and religious beliefs of the American native tribes and the African natives brings to light striking similarities between the two cultures. African religion dramatizes its unity in the universal appeal to the spirits that animate all of nature. Humans, stones, trees, animals, lakes, rivers, and mountains are conjoined in one grand movement toward the continuation of life. However, a closer examination reveals the ideas of reciprocity, circularity, and continuity of the human community which are essential elements in the discourse on African religion. At the core of this continuity is the belief that ancestors remain active in the community of the living. Almost all other actions on Earth are dependent on the eternal community that encompasses the unborn, the living, and the deceased.

African religious beliefs lay a great emphasis on the interconnectedness between the humans and non-human nature. Similar to the Biblical story narrating the Fall of Man, myths recounting man's fallen state can be found in various native cultures. In *Primal Myths*, Barbara C. Sproul explains:

> "*In the West, we are quite familiar with the fall as dramatized in the myth of Adam and Eve. There it seems a matter of acquiring false knowledge of opposites as real. The duality of good and evil, their polar opposition, becomes the central focus and any notion of the unifying sacrality of Being-Itself is lost. Similar explanations for the fall are given in other traditions. African myths, which, more than any others, stress this loss of absoluteness, speak of the fall as the result of man's distinguishing himself from the rest of nature. He rises above the animals and out of the harmony of the natural world to impose his own temporal and essentially evil order on it. Doing so, he forgets the harmony of the divine order and, as the myths put it symbolically, drives God away from the earth. (31)*"

Africa has a long and rich oral tradition that survives to this day. Cultural beliefs, traditions, histories, myths, legends, and rules for living have been passed down orally from generation to generation. The keepers of the oral tradition are bards—tribal poet-singers and storytellers. Bards are charged with remembering and passing along a culture's history and tradition through story and song. Almost all existing epics come from recordings of live performances by African bards. Because they are part of an oral tradition, African myths and legends are flexible and creative, depending on who is telling the story and why. Tribal elders may use a particular legend to teach religious beliefs or reinforce proper behaviour, while children often tell the same stories for their own amusement. For example, a storyteller who wants to warn children about the dangers of wandering off may tell a folk tale in which a disobedient child is shredded to bits by a sharp-toothed lion. Choosing the same tale to teach mothers to keep track of their children, the storyteller might create a character of a foolish mother whose laziness is responsible for her child being eaten by the lion. A child who tells the same story to a group of friends might want to emphasize how clever children are, making the disobedient child outsmart the lion by doing something silly, like farting in its face to get away. An adult telling the same story might show the father saving the child from the lion by diverting the lion's attention with a whistle.

Animals and elements of nature are important cultural and religious symbols for the African tribes. The belief in spirits governing animate and inanimate things is predominant among the tribes. In Africa, the world exists as a place full of energy, dynamism, and life, and the holding back of chaos by harmonizing the spirit world is the principal task of the human being in keeping with nature. In the African world, spirits exist. This is not a debatable issue in most African societies. The existence of spirits that are employed in the maintenance of balance and harmony represents the continuous search for equilibrium.

What is believed intensely all over the continent of Africa is that the Supreme Being, who could be male, female, or both, created the universe, animals, and human beings, but soon retreated from any direct involvement in the affairs of humans. In some cases, in Africa, the Supreme Being does not finish the creation; it is left to other deities to complete. Among the Yoruba, this delegation of creation appears when Olorun, the Owner of the Sky, the Supreme God, starts the creation of the universe and then leaves it to Obatala, a lesser deity, to complete the task. Among the Herero of Namibia, the Supreme God, Omukuru, the Great One, Njambi Kurunga, withdrew into the sky after creating lesser divinities and humans. There are neither temples nor shrines to the God of Gods among most people in Africa. In most cases, the lesser divinities are worshipped, revered, loved, and feared.

Among the Bushmen, Cagn was the first being who created other life forms. He was responsible for the creation of sun, moon, stars, plants and animals. Barbara C. Sproul writes:

> "*... he gave orders and caused all things to appear, and to be made, the sun, the moon, stars, wind, mountains, and animals. His wife's name was Coti. He had two sons, and the eldest was chief, and his name was Cogaz; the name of the second was Gewi.... He was at that time making all animals and things, and making them fit for the use of men, and making snares and weapons. He made then the partridge and the striped mouse, and he made the wind in order that game*

should smell up the wind—so they run up the wind still.... (38)"

The Barotse or Lozi people of Zambia tell of a harmonious and sacred beginning when the creator Nyambi lived on earth with his wife and made all things. Because of man's transgression—he murdered other creatures—Nyambi first banished him from his sacred realm; later he forgave his errant creature and presented him with land to till, but Kamonu reverted to his old ways. Finally, in despair, Nyambi retreated from the world.

Aside from asserting the appropriateness of farming as an occupation in harmony with the sacred way of the world and describing the disruption of that harmony caused by hunting, the myth clearly depicts human nature as ambitious and aggressive, at odds with the will of God. Kamonu is more intelligent but less sensible than others, as is evidenced by his final attempt to restore his connection to Nyambi. Having caused the breach, he attempts to repair it by building a great tower to heaven, but his failure shows the irrevocable nature of the split. Cut off from his creator, he can only greet him now as the sun.

The people of Mozambique also recount a myth pretty much similar to the one found in the culture of the Barotse. The Yao live on the shores of Lake Nyasa in northern Mozambique. Unlike many other Bantu tribes who envision a heavenly origin for people, the Yao assert their emergence from the earth, born from a hole in the ground or, as is the case here, from the water. Sproule explains in detail the creation myth of the Yao tribe:

"At First there were no people. Only Mulungu and the decent peaceful beasts were in the world.

One day Chameleon sat weaving a fish-trap, and when he had finished he set it in the river. In the morning he pulled the trap and it was full of fish, which he took home and ate.

He set the trap again. In the morning he pulled it out and it was empty: no fish. "Bad luck," he said, and set the trap again.

The next morning when he pulled the trap he found a little man and woman in it. He had never seen any creatures like this.

"What can they be?" he said. "Today I behold the unknown." And he picked up the fish-trap and took the two creatures to Mulungu.

"Father," said Chameleon, "see what I have brought."

Mulungu looked. "Take them out of the trap," he said. "Put them down on the earth and they will grow."

Chameleon did this. And the man and woman grew. They grew until they became as tall as men and women are today.

All the animals watched to see what the people would do. They made fire. They rubbed two sticks together in a special way and thus made fire. The fire caught in the bush and roared through the forest and the animals had to run to escape the flames. The people caught a buffalo and killed it and roasted it in the fire and ate it. Then next day they did the same thing. Every day they set fires and killed some animal and ate it.

> *"They are burning up everything!" said Mulungu. "They are killing my people!"*
>
> *All the beasts ran into the forest as far away from mankind as they could get.*
>
> *Chameleon went into the high trees.*
>
> *"I'm leaving!" said Mulungu.*
>
> *He called to Spider. "How do you climb on high?" he said.*
>
> *"Very nicely," said Spider. And Spider spun a rope for Mulungu and Mulungu climbed the rope and went to live in the sky. (43-44)*"

The Yao agree, however, with other Africans in their estimation of human character. Peoples' "progress" in controlling their environment, their ability to hunt successfully and to make fires, is seen from the perspective of the rest of nature and its creator as destructive and cruel. Having violated the sacred harmony of the world, people force God to retreat to the sky. All animals are sacred in African religious traditions. They play vital roles in the creation of the heavens, Earth, and people. They bring messages of life, death, social order, customs, and practices. Some are regarded as deities, whereas others represent deities. On a practical level, animals provide food for humans and are a source of social wealth and standing. Through totems, they also distinguish relations among members of a particular community. For this reason, the images of animals, whether it be in stories or on textiles, houses, temples, shrines, pots, containers, drums, and sculptures, impart a sense of the sacred to the everyday and ritual life of Africans.

Many African stories hold that long ago people and animals could communicate and that individuals in some cultures were able to become one with specific animals. Over time, this ability was lost to most people except for select specialists such as hunters, healers, shaman, priests, or priestesses. Although communication was no longer possible, reverence remained. Animals, because of their complex human-like activities, were early teachers of humans, in the sense that humans learned from watching animal behaviour. By observing their behaviour, Africans were able to discover in-depth information about themselves and their world. These animals then became symbols, and their images were used to convey important information.

Their connection to the natural world motivated the ancient Africans to identify themselves with animal totems that best fit or embodied the power or ability of that particular animal. The ancient Africans paid their respect to and held animals in high regard because they believed that specific animals possessed certain characteristics or features of the gods who revered them. It was one of the ways that the divine could manifest itself for human perception and understanding.

The animals chosen as totems reflected the Africans' understanding of themselves and their connection to nature. Africans also regarded animals as an archetype or aspect of an incarnate god. The animals were not God, but a representation or aspect of it and similarly associated with the Ba (spirit/soul) on Earth. Their high esteem for animals went so far as to be associated with divinity. Gods and human beings in the future life had the ability to shape-shift or transform into any animal or other life form whenever they desired. It is this intimate respect that led them to mummify and treat the body of the deceased animal like that of a human body for the same purpose of afterlife and immortality. This philosophy is directly tied to their understanding of God and the mobility of the soul after death.

In the religious beliefs and cultural practices of the native Americans and the African tribes, non-human life forms and the environment assume positions of significance. The myths, legends, folklore and oral tales handed down from generation to generation reiterate the necessity to preserve the delicate relationship between the human community and non-human nature. The timeless nature of the myths, cultural beliefs and religions of the natives displayed an innate sense of understanding about the vital importance of nature and ecology in the daily lives of the humans. The myths sufficiently illustrated the fact that man was not a separate entity present outside the natural world; he was very much a part of the ecology and had a role to play in preserving the ecological balance.

The beliefs and practices of the native tribes of America and Africa were contrary to the views and ideologies espoused by the colonisers and settlers. The Europeans espoused anthropocentric worldviews and treated non-human nature as the 'other'. They perceived the ecology in terms of resources designed for human consumption. Anthropocentrism was responsible for the alienation of the human community from the ecology and non-human nature. Native tribes who shared an intimate relationship with the ecology became the victims of the anthropocentric mindset of the European settlers. Colonisation earned notoriety for its exploitive practices that marginalised and alienated the ecology and native tribes. The myths of the natives which narrated the deep sense of belongingness with the natural world were branded as primitive and savage tales by the colonising powers.

CHAPTER FIVE

MYTHS, CULTURES AND COEXISTENCE

According to the *Isha Upanishad*, "The entire universe and everything in it, animate and inanimate, is His. Let us not covet anything. Let us treat everything around us reverently, as custodians. We have no charter for dominion. All wealth is commonwealth. Let us enjoy but neither hoard nor kill. The humble frog has as much right to live as we". As the above words from the *Isha Upanishad* suggests, the Oriental and Aboriginal traditions proclaim a deep respect for nature and its animals.

The almost universal message is that, in contrast with Aboriginal and Oriental identity with nature, the West has set out to dominate nature and manipulate it for solely human ends. For example, in his *An Unnatural Order: Uncovering the Roots of Our Domination of Nature and Each Other,* Jim Mason argues that animal cruelty is a quintessential aspect of Western culture fed by the same source as its racism, sexism, and elitism. For Mason, that source of oppression is the Western form of agriculture. He fails to acknowledge the abundant racism, sexism, and elitism of non-Western societies, including tribal and hunting societies. Indeed, he depicts pre-agricultural societies idyllically as belonging to "A World Alive and Ensouled." We have to wonder why there is no mention of slavery in hunting societies, of the denial of the right of worship to women in some tribal societies, or of the caste system. Where overwhelming evidence requires that we acknowledge what Mason calls "dominionism" in other cultures, he still insists that the West "is the primary culprit" and, where dominionism is present in other cultures, it is "rather less rampant and often diluted."

For as long as human beings have practiced them, the complex and multifaceted beliefs, rituals, and moral teachings known as religion have told us how to think about and relate to everything on earth that we did not make ourselves. Whether as “nature,” “creation,” the “ten thousand things,” or “all our relations,” humanity’s surroundings were both a gift and a problem. Because they were the source of our sustenance, a source for which we clearly were not responsible, they were a gift. Because we had to think about what they meant morally and spiritually, and because while we had to use them to meet our needs, t often seemed intuitively clear that in some sense these other beings had their own integrity, purposefulness, and value, they were a problem.

In other religious traditions the distinction between humans and nature was not nearly so clear. Indigenous traditions for the most part saw the natural world as “peopled” by beings with whom it was necessary to cultivate mutually respectful relationships. Daoism viewed humans as an essential part of nature, eschewing as well any fixed distinction between the mind or soul and the body. In Hinduism the entire universe is God, and for Buddhism reincarnation as an animal in a future life is fully compatible with being a human in this one. And in any case the goal of a realized Buddhist (at least in the Mahayana tradition) was to ease the suffering of "all sentient beings," not just of people. Often, however, this more encouraging metaphysical attitude was unaccompanied by actual care for the natural world—and in any case Eastern religions did not have much of a prophetic tradition with which to galvanize adherents to socially critical responses to injustice to people or nature. And with the advent of modernity (or perhaps much earlier) indigenous traditions were marginalized by modern states.

Global climate change has already damaged, and will damage at an increasing rate, agriculture, wild lands, and animals; raise the ocean level and precipitate more intense storms and worse draughts; expand the range of tropical insects and diseases and kill coral; and in all likelihood have effects that we cannot foresee. A staggering accumulation of chemical, heavy metal, biological, and nuclear wastes is found in every region, no matter how remote, and leads to a plague of environmentally caused diseases—most obviously the dramatic increase in cancer, immune-system problems, and birth defects.

From overuse of chemical agriculture and the destruction of forests, the loss of topsoil threatens the production of food throughout the developing nations and leads to erosion and desertification everywhere. Massive erosion can also destroy ecosystem balance in rivers and coastal fishing areas. In what some call a crisis of biodiversity, the decimation of habitats through expanding human settlements, logging, mining, agriculture, and pollution and the killing of animals for sport, use, or food have raised rates of extinction to the highest they have been for sixty-five million years. Potential medicines vanish, ecosystems are destabilized, water supplies threatened, and irreplaceable natural beauties are lost forever. As we witness the harm we are doing we also lose ethical confidence in humanity's own worth. Loss of wilderness is seen in the increasing rarity of ecosystems that are free to develop without human interference or intrusion. Besides the dwindling of biodiversity that this entails, human beings face a paradoxical loneliness.

People are everywhere; yet we are haunted by a deep loneliness for those natural others who have been our companions for biological ages. The last examples of human communities integrated into nonhuman nature are giving way to devastation of indigenous peoples. As their environments are poisoned, native peoples lose their land and culture and too often their lives. Unsustainable patterns and quantities of consumption deplete natural resources and contribute to global warming and the accumulation of waste. In the underdeveloped world, overpopulation relative to existing technological resources and political organization decimates the landscape. Genetic engineering menaces us with the dismal prospects of engineered lifeforms and the potentially catastrophic invention of insufficiently tested organisms. Given our track record with nuclear wastes and toxic chemicals and our political and economic elites' pronounced tendency to shortsightedness and greed, it seems highly doubtful that we are ready to create new life-forms in a cautious and sensible way.

The sheer scope of this crisis means that *nature*—however it was thought of before this time—has been transformed into something new: the *environment*, that is, a nonhuman world whose life and death, current shape and future prospects, are in large measure determined by human beings. If the rest of the universe is beyond our reach, the earth— or at least the earth's atmosphere, surface, waters, and ecosystems—plainly is not. In a sense modern industry, development, land use, and technology means that if a clear-cut distinction between nature and people was ever possible, it is so no longer. Human beings and the environment now form a dialectical totality, each side affecting, and being affected by, the other. If we still depend on nature for food and water, air and minerals, every wild ecosystem depends on some political arrangement for protection, and every living thing is affected by human-made climate change, importation of exotic species, habitat loss, and pollution.

If the environmental crisis represents both a deep obligation for religious response and an important opportunity for a specifically religious contribution, it is also the case that environmental movements are by their very nature hospitable to religion. This is because environmentalism (though, of course, not without some very unpleasant exceptions) tends to have a spiritual dimension which other liberal or leftist political movements lack. Compared to often partial and partisan struggles for democracy, in support of rights for workers, women, or racial minorities, against colonialism, or for more economic justice, environmentalism bears remarkable and crucially important affinities with religion. These affinities make the emerging alliance between secular environmental organizations and institutional religion particularly appropriate; and they mean that at times it is quite difficult to talk about the "relations" between religion and environmentalism since the two so shade together that it becomes hard to tell them apart.

In the contemporary environmental movement even those groups totally unconnected to religiously identified organizations are often inspired by a political ideology, or at least by a moral sensibility, with powerful religious overtones. This sensibility has been present in much environmentalism since its origins in the mid-nineteenth century and has evolved into a comprehensive worldview which in many respects is often undeniably spiritual in nature.

These claims are supported by the fact that much of early conservationism itself emerged from a religious sense of the earth as God's creation, a "temple" that we should not despoil. Thus, in the initial years of conservation leading voices as disparate as Thoreau, John Muir, Robert Marshall, Sigurd Olson, and John Burroughs celebrated nature not only for its physical beauty and utility, but for its spiritual value as well. As historian Michael P. Nelson observes, it is quite common for people to argue for the preservation of wilderness as a "a site for spiritual, mystical, or religious encounters: places to experience mystery, moral regeneration, spiritual revival, meaning, oneness, unity, wonder, awe, inspiration, or a sense of harmony with the rest of creation—all essential religious experiences." According to Llewelyn Vaughan-Lee:

> "*The world is not a problem to be solved; it is a living being to which we belong. The world is part*

of our own self and we are a part of its suffering wholeness. Until we go to the root of our image of separateness, there can be no healing. And the deepest part of our separateness from creation lies in our forgetfulness of its sacred nature, which is also our own sacred nature. When our Western monotheistic culture suppressed the many gods and goddesses of creation, cut down the sacred groves and banished God to heaven, we began a cycle that has left us with a world destitute of the sacred, in a way unthinkable to any indigenous people. The natural world and the people who carry its wisdom know that the created world and all of its many inhabitants are sacred and belong together. Our separation from the natural world may have given us the fruits of technology and science, but it has left us bereft of any instinctual connection to the spiritual dimension of life—the connection between our soul and the soul of the world, the knowing that we are all part of one living, spiritual being. (13)"

It is this wholeness that is calling to us now, that needs our response. It needs us to return to our own root and rootedness: our relationship to the sacred within creation. Only from the place of sacred wholeness and reverence can we begin the work of healing, of bringing the world back into balance.

Environmental knowledge and accompanying practices in all societies are closely associated with other widely held values about how people understand the world and their place in it. Even though these values change with new knowledge and new technologies, we can still speak with confidence about culturally specific systems. A society's views on nature and the environment arise from and reflect its cultural beliefs and customs. At the same time, for centuries if not millennia there have been exchanges and cross-fertilization among environmental systems around the world.

All people everywhere transform nature. This is the case with huge industrial societies and with small hunting-gathering ones. The scales may be different, but people need to make use of the land and water to survive. Hunter-gatherers burned the forest to make it easier to find game and to encourage certain species. Some Native American cultures killed more buffalo than they could possibly eat or use. Early agricultural societies dammed rivers and irrigated. These practices were not necessarily harmful to the land – much of the latest evidence shows that controlled burning in many societies, such as in Aboriginal Australia, encouraged biodiversity and prevented large uncontrolled burns by keeping the understory low and limiting the fuel available to burn. At the same time, it is clear that practices like these are what we now call ecologically sound, even though the cultures using them did not always articulate the practices in anything like philosophical terms.

Human beings share with many other social animals the ability to discriminate between one's own and other groups, but to legitimize this distinction in terms of moral evaluation is probably uniquely human. The Other has always been important in order not only to define ourselves as human beings – whether the Other is defined biologically, socially, spatially or temporally– but also to put forward claims of a moral order.

Many earlier peoples saw in the natural phenomena a world beyond ephemeral appearance, an abiding world, a world imaged forth in the wonders of the sun and clouds by day and the stars and planets by night, a world that enfolded the human in some profound manner. This other world was guardian, teacher, healer—the source from which humans were born, nourished, protected, guided, and the destiny to which we returned. This led to the creation of the different myths across various cultures, and these myths largely hinged on a respect and reverence towards the natural world.

Following the Renaissance and the Industrial Revolution, Western thinkers and philosophers adopted a mechanistic stance towards nature and ecology. It was based on anthropocentrism that rejected the theocentric and ecocentric beliefs of the past. According to Rob Boddice:

> "*Anthropocentrism is expressed either as a charge of human chauvinism, or as an acknowledgement of human ontological boundaries. It is in tension with nature, the environment and non-human animals (as well as non-humans per se). It is in apparent contrast to other-worldly cosmologies, religions and philosophies. Anthropocentrism has provided order and structure to humans' understanding of the world, while unavoidably expressing the limits of that understanding. It influences our ethics, our politics, and the moral status of Others. Yet these expressions leave some doubt about the extent to which the concept and its history are*

understood. (1)"

The sanctity of life, or of nature, entails a knowledge of the sacred, which too cannot escape the confines of human construction. In short, any ethical, value-based, law-based, or society-based view of the world is inherently and irredeemably anthropocentric. This seems implausible because the process of acquiring these world perspectives is to us invisible, and we therefore operate with and within them, unaware that we overlay cosmology with ideology at every step. We are alienated from our categories of analysis precisely because, as Latour says, 'the notions of nature and politics had been developed over centuries'. They are fundamentally *ours*, and we make good use of them; but we should not expect the outcomes of analyses so carried out to be anything other than *human*.

Philosophers in the West conceptualize the human condition as a middle station between animality and divinity and maintain that of all earthly beings, human beings are closest to the gods. This prejudice persists even in Kant's cosmopolitanism, in which human beings stand alone among earthly beings as capable of perfecting their natures and achieving the status of "lords of nature." Standing in close proximity to the gods gives human beings license to exercise lordship over animals and other created beings. To call our representations of the gods into question is to challenge our privileged status as lords of nature.

Anthropocentrism literally means human-centered, and it refers to the tendency whereby humans judge the importance and interests of other animals by their importance and interest to humans. It also refers to the fact that any knowledge we have of the world, and by implication of other animals in it, is mediated through a human perspective. Anthropocentric worldviews have a long history and are, arguably, the main way in which we see and interpret the world today. Unfortunately, this has several negative consequences for animals as they become defined only according to human importance and/or interests. For example, we have animal welfare statutes in various countries that protect those animals we deem worthy of protection, such as companion animals, but only do so as a form of property. In other words, their standing within the legal system is determined by their relationship to us. If we do not "own" them or do not deem them important, then their level of protection drops or becomes non-existent. Thus, farm animals are accorded importance *only* as stock and not as individual animals. Similarly, cruelty to companion animals is processed by those in the criminal justice system as a matter of damage to property, so recompense comes to the human at hand for property lost, and sentences remain light for those who deliberately harm animals because they are not considered sentient beings.

Ecocentrism developed as an antithesis to anthropocentrism. Instead of privileging the human point of view, as in anthropocentric accounts of the world, ecocentric accounts seek to decenter humanity and instead recenter nature. In other words, nature is seen as having intrinsic value, value beyond that which it offers to humans. Ecocentric interpretations of the world are not particularly new and were in fact rife during the late 1970s and '80s when ecofeminists such as Carolyn Merchant sought to rethink human–nature relations. Merchant opened *The Death of Nature* with the statement that "The world we have lost was organic". And from here she went on to develop the argument that between approximately 1500 to 1700, Western worldviews have moved from organic to mechanistic stances. With this change in belief came a change in behaviour, as previous organic worldviews had built into them prohibitions against simply using the earth as a resource.

As Merchant carefully describes, there was a move away from organic worldviews which presumed the interrelatedness of humans, animals, and nature to a mechanistic worldview, which was predicated on their separation and thus allowed and facilitated their manipulation and control. Increasingly, scientific and technological rationalism gained ascendancy, and in this framework, nature was something to be controlled. Human civility could be proven by demarcating our distance from "the beasts" and from nature itself, and thus it became a right and indeed a necessity for humans to make use of the resources the natural world offered. This intellectual legacy is one that is still prevalent today.

In many discussions concerning the nature of humans and society, a principled distinction is assumed between humans and animals. The characteristics that are taken to be fundamental to human beings and the social life they lead are precisely those that distinguish them from animals, and thus make the human world different from the animal world. Notwithstanding the emergence of Darwinian theory, which points to the mental and physical continuity between humans and other animals, this assumed distinction between the human realm and that of the natural realm, which includes animals, is a persistent theme in social thought.

Perhaps the greatest of the many ethical problems faced by human beings at the beginning of a new millennium is deciding the extent to which we are entitled to alter the natural world for our convenience. Unprecedented capabilities such as genetic engineering and the harnessing of atomic energy give us far more power than wisdom. The idea of every animal as a tradition will not give us a simple answer to our dilemmas, but it will at least provide a way in which to think of them. Traditions tend to degenerate when they are not adjusted to changing conditions, but alterations are generally made in a cautious and respectful manner. To preserve an animal as a tradition, we must know it intimately, we must be familiar with the lore that has grown up around the creature since time immemorial.

In tribal societies, human form is not always important. All beings are forever changing their shapes, like waves breaking on the shore. Human beings may become ravens, while hares may turn into human beings. You become what you eat; you become what you are eaten by. Death is simply a transition, a bit like the passage from girl to woman or boy to man.

Totems are animals from which a tribe traces its ancestry. Beyond that, they are guardians of the tribe, at times revisiting the members in trances or in dreams. Among the Indo-Europeans, the tribal totem was perhaps most frequently the wolf. Going into battle, warriors would be possessed by the spirit of the wolf, and our legends of werewolves are a legacy of that archaic time. A mother wolf suckled Romulus and Remus, the legendary founders of Rome; a woodpecker fed them. Among people of the Far North, totems were most often birds. For the Native Americans of the Northwest coast, the favorite totem was frequently the raven, sometimes the bear; for tribes farther south, it might have been the coyote, beaver, or jaguar. Legends of totemistic societies commemorate learning the arts of civilization from observation of animals. The Navaho Indians, for example, tell how women learned to weave from Spider Woman. Other stories may tell of learning to build from beavers or to hunt from wolves. Traditional dances often imitate the motions of animals, while music sometimes mimics their sounds. Observing what bears or snakes would eat has revealed many herbal medicines. Concerning the intimate relationship between humans and non-humans in prehistoric cultures, Boria Sax explains:

> "*The prehistoric cave paintings of France and Spain are among the most ancient works of art that we have. The human beings in these paintings are usually crude stick figures that the artists must not have considered very important. The animals are painted with far more care and passion. The first clearly identifiable religious shrines in history are at Çatal Hüyük in Anatolia and date from around the middle of the seventh millennium A.D. They were dedicated to animals, especially bulls, but also vultures, foxes, and others. The ancient Egyptians believed their creator god Ptah was incarnated in a bull named Apis that could be recognized by specific markings. Apis was kept in a temple and honored in sacred rites. The Egyptians also worshipped their gods as incarnated in cats, ibises, and many other creatures. (xiii-xiv)*"

Over millennia, anthropomorphic goddesses and gods slowly replaced the animal deities. The archaic divinities accompanied their more human successors, often as mascots or alternate forms. Athena, for example, was pictured with an owl, Zeus with an eagle; Odin was accompanied by ravens and by wolves; Mary, mother of Christ, was often shown with a dove.

As tribes were absorbed into kingdoms and empires, their religions were fused and local deities were combined. Archaic practices sometimes continued as local cults or customs. In Rome, people would sometimes keep snakes in their homes, believing it the spirit of an ancestor. This practice survived into modern times in parts of Italy. A few holy men and women retained the shaman's gift of speaking with creatures of the woods and fields. Saint Francis preached to the birds, while Saint Anthony evangelized the fish. Figures that blend human and animal features became common with the transition from hunting and gathering to agriculture. The gods and goddesses of ancient Egypt often had a human torso and the head of an animal—crocodile, baboon, jackal, cat, falcon, or ibis.

Central to the religious beliefs of the ancient Egyptians was the myth of Isis and Osiris, in which Isis's husband, Osiris, is killed by their evil brother Set, who tricks Osiris into climbing into a box. Osiris is sealed in the box and dies when it is thrown into the Nile. Isis, the bereaved wife, searches for and finds the body of her dead husband and is determined to give him a proper burial on Egyptian soil. It is from this myth that the crucial elements of Egyptian funerary practices derived. Like all myths, this one revealed important truths about nature, the universe, and life after death, and many beliefs of the ancient Egyptian funerary cult can be derived from it. The chest that exactly fit Osiris was the precursor of the anthropoid coffin, which is shaped like the deceased and is intended to protect the body. The importance of a proper burial on Egyptian soil is emphasized by the efforts that Isis made to find the body of her husband, and to make sure that it was complete, so that when she spoke her magic words, Osiris would resurrect in the Netherworld. He kept the same body after death that he had during life, so mummification was essential if the deceased was to resurrect and spend eternity in the Netherworld.

Animals played a big part in the mythology and religion of ancient Egypt. Some animals were associated with or sacred to the gods, but animals themselves were not worshipped. While the falcon was the symbol of Horus and the cat was the symbol of Bastet, for example, the Egyptians did not worship every falcon and cat or believe these animals were gods. Some animals sacred to the gods were raised on farms specifically to be killed and mummified and sold to people who made pilgrimages to the temples. The faithful could purchase a mummified cat, ibis, or falcon and present it to the god as a votive offering in the hope that their prayers would be answered. Some animals, however, were designated as the living embodiments of a god. The Egyptians believed a god could inhabit the body of a particular falcon, and that falcon would be considered a living cult image. As the living representation of the god, that falcon would be worshipped as if he were the actual god, Horus. Particularly during the Late and Ptolemaic periods, any animal in which the spirit of the god was believed to dwell was housed in luxury in the temple precincts. The many different manifestations of the gods included the ram of Amun, the ibis of Thoth, the crocodile of Sobek, and the falcon in various forms of Horus, to mention a few.

The faithful had various ways to identify which animal a spirit inhabited. During one ceremony to determine which animal would represent the god, the cult statue, carried by the priests, would seem to dip toward a particular animal. Each year a new living manifestation of the god was chosen and installed in the temple precinct with a great deal of pomp and ceremony. The fate of the deposed animal is not known. Some animals, like the Apis, Buchis, and Mnevis bulls, were chosen for their special markings. They were selected after an exhaustive search that began when the previous bull died. Once found, the bull travelled to its new home in the temple to be installed with great ceremony as the living manifestation of Apis, Buchis, or Mnevis, an honour it would hold for the rest of its life. When a bull died, Egypt went into mourning. The bull was mummified and placed in a tomb fit for a head of state. According to Lewis Spence:

> "*It is obvious, for example, that the cat-headed Bast, who was worshipped first in the shape of a cat, was originally a cat totem. The crocodile was the incarnation of the god Sebek, and dwelt in a lake near Krokodilopolis. Ra and Horus are represented with the heads of hawks, and Thoth with the head of an ibis. Anubis has the head of a jackal. That some of these forms are totemic is not open to doubt. But it was a decadent totemism, in which the more primitive sentiment*

> *was focused on particular animals considered as divine, totems which had become full-fledged divinities. (10-11)*"

The inspiring cause of animal-worship was undoubtedly at first nothing more or less than fear, with an admixture of awesome admiration of the creature's excelling power and strength. Later there developed the idea of animals as typifying gods, the actual embodiments of divine and superhuman attributes. Thus the bull and the ram, possessors of exceptional procreative energy, came to represent gods of nature and the phenomena of yearly rejuvenescence.

Greek authors focus primarily on the city and its festivals, yet most Greeks were peasants who lived in the countryside and supported the towns through farming and herding. The experience of this majority certainly included a much closer acquaintance with the gods of the landscape than our literary sources suggest.

The category of "nature deities" is a modern construct. All of the Greek gods were connected in one way or another with natural phenomena, so in some sense all are nature deities. Zeus was a god of rain, Poseidon of earthquakes, Artemis of wild beasts. Even deities like Athena whose panhellenic personae were focused on the cultural rather than the natural sphere could be called upon in a variety of contexts to influence natural processes, such as stopping a plague or helping to ensure good crops. A number of lesser deities, however, were nature gods in the sense that they personified specific features in the landscape or phenomena in the environment. They will be the subject of this chapter.

In terms of the audience of prospective worshipers, these deities fall into two groups. First are the innumerable gods of the rivers and springs, mountains and lakes. While myths of the river gods and nymphs occasionally became known to a panhellenic audience, their cults were geographically limited to a particular town or region. In this respect, they were like the heroes and heroines, and made a similar contribution to the self-definition of the communities who worshiped them. The second group is comprised of divine entities perceived and recognized by all: the deities representing the earth, sun, moon, sea, and winds. Among the classical Greeks, these aspects of the environment were everywhere recognized as divine, but their myths and cults remained undeveloped relative to those of the more complex Olympians and the more numerous local gods.

The nineteenth-century concept of the "vegetation god" does not correspond to any individual member of the Greek pantheon; instead, many Greek gods, including the nymphs, included growing things among their spheres of influence. Similarly, many gods regulated the animal world. Among these, Pan will be treated because he alone is a Master of Animals who himself partakes of animal form and nature as a regular part of his panhellenic persona. According to Daniel Ogden:

> "*Another important issue in the relationship between nature and Greek religion has to do with the environment of worship, the context in which people encountered their gods. While every city had its intramural sanctuaries, the Greeks never stopped visiting and building places of worship in the countryside, often in remote and inaccessible*

locations. The panhellenic construct of Olympus as the home of the gods existed in tension with cult practice, which located the gods in their sanctuaries and viewed the altar and the cult statue as the places where the gods were most predictably manifest and present. (57)"

Mountain peaks, groves, springs, caves, and other landscape features were often regarded as inherently sacred, and their symbolic fascination was closely bound up with their aesthetic appeal. Territorial and economic reasons for the placement of sanctuaries certainly existed, and strategic placement helps to account for the spectacular success of individual sanctuaries.

Hinduism through the myths and ritualistic practices underscored the relationship between the human community and the natural world. The myths, philosophical beliefs and cultural practices went a long way in presenting man's position in the natural world- he was very much a part of the ecology. "Every aspect of (her) life is intimately connected with nature and the environment, and scientific environmental management" (Krishna 9). Explaining the importance of nature Nanditha Krishna explains:

"*The verses of the Vedas express a deep sense of communion of man with god. Nature is a friend, revered as a mother, obeyed as a father and nurtured as a beloved child. It is sacred because man depends on it and because of this everything is sanctified, including man and the terrifying aspects of nature, such as landslides, earthquakes and storms. Natural phenomena are the*

> *manifestations or expressions of the gods and not the gods themselves. They express the principles that govern the world and the cosmic order, rita. (10)"*

Hindu myths and cultural practices have largely rested on coexistence between humans and non-human nature including the various other life forms. "In Vedic literature, all of nature was, in some way, divine, part of an indivisible life force uniting the world of humans, animals and plants" (Krishna 11).

Like Hinduism, Buddhism has also maintained the coexistence between humans and the natural world. Buddhist myths, rituals and cultural practices espouse the belief in non-violence and compassion towards other life forms and the environment. The Jataka tales and stories about Boddhisattva frequently feature animals and birds. They have divine attributes and are in no way inferior to humans. S. Dhammika explains:

> *"Like any sensitive person, the Buddha was fascinated by the diversity of the natural world he saw around him. He commented: 'I know of no other type of living beings as diverse as those of the animal kingdom'. This awareness of and sensitivity to animals meant that he took them into account in his Dhamma, particularly in his cosmology and his ethics. (8)"*

In India, the belief in the supreme being as a manifestation of the entire nature has been at the core of the harmony with the environment. The supreme being was present in all aspects of nature and the humans learnt to revere the natural world. According to Nanditha Krishna:

> *"The Supreme Being or Brahman is the underlying power of unity, pervading all creation: forests and groves, trees and plants, animals, rivers, waterbodies, mountains, gardens, towns and precincts and seeds. Nature is venerated all over India. Every village has a sacred grove presided over by a local deity; every temple has a sacred garden and sacred tree; rivers and lakes are revered; and mountains are the dwelling place of the gods. Nature is a manifestation of the divine. (17)"*

Western philosophical outlook rooted in anthropocentrism was responsible for repudiating the intimate relationship between the humans and non-human nature. Largely based on a system of control and dominance, anthropocentrism was responsible for causing enormous strain to the ecology. The myths, religious beliefs and cultural practices of marginalized and primitive communities have often been at the forefront of coexisting harmoniously with the ecology. Colonialism has painted the indigenous communities along with their rituals, myths and religious beliefs as savage and barbaric.

The Europeans viewed the native tribes with mistrust and suspicion, labelling them as primitive, barbaric and akin to animals. This was the justification on the part of the colonising forces to use brute force against the natives to subjugate them and destroy their culture. The biggest testimony to the colonial barbarism is the utter annihilation of the Mayan civilisation. Hernan Cortes invaded Tenochtitlan and essayed the destruction of a remarkable civilisation and subjugated the Mayans. Tales of fabled riches had reached the Europeans which led the Conquistadors to conquer the Mayan civilisation; similar tales of riches and resources led the colonial powers to conquer the continents of Asia and Africa. The East had attracted the Europeans for long due to its spices, silk and jewels. Africa- labelled as the dark continent came as a surprise to the settlers who began to tap into the natural resources, minerals, metals, gem stones and ivory. The natives who resisted the settlers and imperial powers were crushed and subsequently marginalised. Colonial powers justified their actions by asserting that they had a moral and religious obligation to take over the land and culture of the native people. Indigenous tribes and natives were forced to bend to the will of the colonising powers; others had to retreat into remote areas to preserve their cultural practices. The subjugation of the native tribes wasn't merely in physical terms; it was also an ideological one. The narrative was created by the imperial powers promoting European supremacy; ultimately the purpose of the narrative was to project the native tribes as barbaric, primitive and savage who needed to be civilised by the Europeans. What unfolded has been aptly summed up by Adele Nozedar:

> "*The striving for cultural superiority—and the many ways and means in which that superiority was demonstrated—has destroyed many lives, crushed cultures and belief systems, wrecked families, and smashed peace and equanimity to smithereens. And yet, ironically, what we perceive*

> *as the Native American way of life is something to which many aspire. The spirituality of the Native American way is not separate from "normal" life as it is for those of a Western mind-set. The innate respect for all of nature, and the consequences of that respect, are goals that have a practical as well as spiritual force and are within reach of everyone, no matter their culture. (6)"*

A policy that was actively encouraged by the white settlers in order to encourage Native Americans to be absorbed into the "mainstream" culture. Assimilation of Natives into the ways of the white man generally resulted in the exchange of one culture for the other; for example, when they were sent to European schools, Native American children were not allowed to use their native tongue, and were encouraged to reject their traditional religious practices in favour of Christian ones. The movement toward assimilation was at its height in the late 1800s and the early 1900s.

Missionaries and colonisers in Africa also employed similar practices. Forcible conversions were carried out and the native African tribes were forced to give up their cultural beliefs, practices and even their native language. They were forced to give up their native languages, cultures and beliefs and conform to the system imposed by the imperial powers. The motive of the colonisers was the political and ideological subjugation of the native tries. They were continually made to believe that their indigenous cultures were inferior to the European one. Missionaries and officials relentlessly worked to ensure that the natives abandoned their own religious beliefs, languages and cultures; conversion and linguistic imperialism were some of the few tools employed by the colonisers to assimilate the native tribes into mainstream culture at the expense of their own cultural uniqueness.

Since time immemorial, the tribes had been practicing their religious beliefs and shaping their culture in accordance with the ecology, non-human nature, environment and wildlife. According to Jon E. Lewis, "As the tribes built relationships with their land, so they themselves changed, in shape, culture, religion, and tongue" (14). Their myths, legends, folklore have also assumed shape under the influence of nature. It was not uncommon on the part of the native tribes to revere the ecology and non-human nature through their religion and cultural practices. But colonialism and imperialism marginalised them, forcing them to abandon their distinctive cultural identity and conform to the framework laid down by the imperialist forces. This led to the endangerment of various indigenous cultures, languages and religious beliefs that had coexisted harmoniously with the natural world.

CHAPTER SIX

CONCLUSION

The ancient identity of nature as a nurturing mother links human history with the history of the environment and ecological change. The female earth was central to the organic cosmology that was undermined by the Scientific Revolution and the rise of a market-oriented culture in early modern Europe. The ecology movement has reawakened interest in the values and concepts associated historically with the premodern organic world. The ecological model and its associated ethics make possible a fresh and critical interpretation of the rise of modern science in the crucial period when our cosmos ceased to be viewed as an organism and became instead a machine.

Deep Ecology and other ecological movements are sharply critical of the costs of competition, aggression, and domination arising from the market economy's *modus operandi* in nature and society. Ecology has been a subversive science in its criticism of the consequences of uncontrolled growth associated with capitalism, technology, and progress-concepts that over the last two hundred years have been treated with reverence in Western culture. The vision of the ecology movement has been to restore the balance of nature disrupted by industrialization and overpopulation. It has emphasized the need to live within the cycles of nature, as opposed to the exploitative, linear mentality of forward progress. It focuses on the costs of progress, the limits to growth, the deficiencies of technological decision making, and the urgency of the conservation and recycling of natural resources.

Ecosophy has come across as the latest development in the field of environmental studies and conservation. Ecosophy blends the study of ecology and philosophy in an effort to raise increased awareness about the necessity to preserve the ecology. Environmental movements like Ecosophy and Deep Ecology share similarities with the beliefs of traditional communities and tribes. Contrary to the Western philosophy rooted in anthropocentrism and Cartesianism, traditional beliefs and practices of indigenous communities of Asia, Africa, America and Australia express a deep sense of belonging towards non-human nature.

The belief in ecology and nature on the part of the native communities was a part of their religious and cultural beliefs. Through myths, religious practices and cultural beliefs reverence towards ecology had been reinforced among the community members. Across most of the creation myths recounted by various cultures around the world, nature is the sacred nurturing mother. If she is Gaia for the ancient Greeks, she is Prithvi for the Hindus. Respecting the ecology, land and the earth itself as the sacred mother went a long way in preserving the environment as the individuals learnt to live in harmony with non-human nature; causing damage to the ecology regarded and revered as the sacred mother was inconceivable. "Indian culture is noted for its deep respect for Mother Nature. Even today, ancient traditions, customs and practices continue to flourish in our day-to-day life. Hinduism is noted for its deep respect for all forms of nature and the unique role that each life form plays in the ecology of the earth" (Krishna 22). Religious beliefs and cultural practices play a prominent role in shaping the human community's ties with the ecology. Nanditha Krishna explains:

> "*Religious practices are influenced by local environmental factors which play an important role in determining the relationship between man and god. Religions that consider that nature was created for the benefit of man and that man is the master of nature permit ruthless exploitation of natural resources. Primitive and nature-sensitive cultures always have some tenet in their religion about the sanctity of natural wealth. All religions have their key festivals coinciding with natural phenomena. (23)*"

The sacredness of nature was further reinforced by the animistic beliefs of native communities. Anthropocentrism has been at the forefront in creating the divide between humans and non-human nature and animals in particular. Animals and birds have been treated as the 'other' and exploited by humans, particularly for capital gains. However, things stand differently for the native communities who identify themselves with the ecology. Not only did they revere the earth and nature as the sacred mother, but also learnt to respect the innumerable living beings living within the ecological system. "In the Puranas, killing animals and eating meat were considered to be such heinous crimes that neither prayers nor pilgrimages or bathing in holy rivers would absolve the consumer" (Krishna 126). Among the tribes of Africa and America, it was not uncommon on their part to subscribe to animistic beliefs; tribes would respect the animals and birds, identifying them as embodiments of the natural world. This is completely in contrast to the Western outlook that has given rise to speciesism. It has been responsible for creating the distinct divide between humans and animals. Advocates of speciesism have comfortably ignored Darwin's theory of evolution which showed man's evolution from the apes. Critiquing the Western stance on the divide between humans and non-human species Margo DeMello comments:

> "*In many non-Western societies, nature and animals are not necessarily categories that are easily to the opposite of culture or humans. In fact, many cultures see (or saw) animals as potential clan members, ancestors, separate nations, or intermediaries between the sacred and profane worlds. Many of those cultures share a belief in animism, a worldview that finds that humans, animals, plants, and inanimate objects all may be endowed with spirit. (34)*"

Animals also play a role in the kinship systems of people around the world. For example, many Native American and Australian groups recognize animals as totems—important genealogical figures to whom members of a clan trace their ancestry, and who provide protection. Some Native American cultures also believe that animals and humans share the same culture even though their bodies are different. Animal totems are found in Africa as well; for example, the Kadimu of Kenya believe that they are descended from pythons. Other cultures believe that the souls or spirits of the dead are incarnated in animals. For instance, the Thai believe that white elephants may contain the souls of the dead, and among the Zulu, Kafirs, Masai, and Nandi of Africa, the snake is seen as the incarnation of dead ancestors. The sacredness of animals achieves great importance in Hinduism through the religious beliefs and myths which sustain the relationship between the humans and the ecology. According to Nanditha Krishna:

> "*Many animals are considered the vehicles or vahanas or the companions of the gods, sometimes even gods themselves. The various cultural connections are expressed through myths and religious practices that celebrate nature and natural resources. The worship of each sacred element in nature reveals people's knowledge of the connection between nature and spiritualism, using religion to protect nature. Thus many animals became vahanas or vehicles of gods. (128)*"

This distinction between human and animal became universal throughout the West and was strengthened through social practice and philosophical thought. In Europe in particular, animals were thought to have been created expressly for human exploitation. Nature was considered a force to be subdued, and Christian clergy, going back to Aquinas and the great chain of being, were especially inclined to emphasize that humans were radically different from and superior to all other creatures. With animality posited as something inferior to humankind and as something to be conquered and exploited, early modern Europeans made concerted efforts to maintain distinct boundaries between themselves and animals; upper-class English families did not allow their babies to crawl, for example, because it was seen as animal-like.

This belief in human superiority sanctioned the exploitation of non-human life forms and it has resulted in the loss of many species. The loss of one species can severely alter the ecological balance and the loss of many species can result in irrevocable environmental damage. The human community sees itself as separate and distinct from the natural world without realising that man is very much a part of the ecological system. Traditional wisdom, myths, folklore and religious beliefs had reinforced the relationship between humans and the ecology, based on mutual respect. Amidst growing concerns over environmental damage and loss of ecology, Deep Ecology and other environmental movements have come up with the solutions to sustain the ties with the ecology. The similarities between the Ecosophy and the myths and cultural practices from around the world are striking. This is enough to illustrate the fact that coexistence and reverence is the need of the hour to preserve the ecology and protect the future of the earth.

References

Adams, W.W. *Green Development Environment and Sustainability in a Developing World*. Routledge, 2009.

Adams, W.W. *Green Development Environment and Sustainability in a Developing World*. Routledge, 2009.

Alexander, Hartley Burr. *Native American Mythology*. Dover Publications, INC., 2005.

Anderson, E.N. *Ecologies of the Heart Emotion, Belief, and the Environment*. Oxford University Press, 1996.

Anderson, Graham. *Greek and Roman Folklore: A Handbook*. Greenwood Press, 2006.

Angell, David J.R., Justyn D. Comer and Matthew L.N. Wilkinson eds. *Sustaining Earth*. Macmillan, 1990.

Angell, David J.R., Justyn D. Comer and Matthew L.N. Wilkinson eds. *Sustaining Earth*. Macmillan, 1990.

Angus, Ian. *Facing the Anthropocene*. Monthly Review Press, 2016.

Ann, Martha and Dorothy Myers Imel. *Goddesses in World Mythology*. ABC CLIO, 1993.

Appignanesi, Richard ed. *Introducing Nietzsche*. Icon Books, 2005.

Ariew, Roger, Dennis Des Chene, Douglas M. Jesseph and et al. eds. *Historical Dictionary of Descartes and Cartesian Philosophy*. Rowman and Littlefield 2015.

Ariew, Roger. *Descartes and the First Cartesians*. Oxford University Press, 2014.

Armesto, Felipe Fernandez. *1492 The Year the World Began*. Harper One, 2010.

Armesto, Felipe Fernandez. *Amerigo The Man Who Gave His Name to America*. Random House, 2007.

Armesto, Felipe Fernandez. *Civilizations Culture, Ambition and the Transformation of Nature.* The Free Press, 2001.

Armitage, Duane. *Heidegger and the Death of God Between Plato and Nietzsche.* Palgrave Macmillan, 2017.

Armstrong, Karen. *A Short History of Myth.* Canongate, 2005.

Arnold, Edwin T. and Diane C. Luce eds. *A Cormac McCarthy Companion The Border Trilogy.* University Press of Mississippi, 2001.

Arnold, Edwin T. and Dianne C. Luce eds. *Perspectives on Cormac McCarthy.* University Press of Mississippi, 1999.

Asante, Molefi Kete and Ama Mazama eds. *Encyclopedia of African Religion.* Sage, 2009.

Bacon, Francis. *Advancement of Learning and Novum Organum.* The Colonial Press, 1899.

Baratta, Chris ed. *Environmentalism in the Realm of Science Fiction and Fantasy Literature.* Cambridge Scholars Publishing, 2012.

Barbier, Edward B. *Capitalizing on Nature Ecosystems as Natural Assets.* Cambridge University Press, 2011.

Barillas, William. *The Midwestern Pastoral Place and Landscape in Literature of the American Heartland.* Ohio University Press, 2006.

Barnhill, David Landis and Roger S. Gottlieb eds. *Deep Ecology and World Religions: New Essays on Sacred Ground.* State University of New York Press, 2001.

Barry, John and Robyn Eckersley eds. *The State and the Ecological Crisis.* The MIT Press, 2005.

Bate, Jonathan. *The Song of the Earth.* Picador, 2001.

Beecroft, Alexander. *An Ecology of World Literature From Antiquity to the Present Day.* Verso, 2015.

Beecroft, Alexander. *An Ecology of World Literature From Antiquity to the Present Day.* Verso, 2015.

Berens, E.M. *The Myths and Legends of Ancient Greece and Rome.* Maynard, Merrill & Co, 2009.

Berkes, Fikret. *Sacred Ecology.* Routledge, 2008.

Berlanstein, Lenard R ed. *The Industrial Revolution and Work in Nineteenth Century Europe.* Routledge, 2005.

Biehl, Janet. *Ecology or Catastrophe: The Life of Murray Bookchin.* Oxford University Press, 2015.

Billington, Ray Aleen and Martin Ridge. *Westward Expansion A History of the American Frontier.* University of New Mexico Press, 2001.

Black, Brian. *Nature and the Environment in Twentieth-Century American Life.* Greenwood Press, 2006.

Bleakley, Alan. *The Animalizing Imagination: Totemism, Textuality and Ecocriticism.* Macmillan Press, 2000.

Boddice, Rob ed. *Anthropocentrism Humans, Animals, Environments.* Brill, 2011.

Bookchin, Murray. *The Ecology of Freedom.* Cheshire Books, 1982.

Bovenkerk, Bernice and Jozef Keulartz eds. *Animal Ethics in the Age of Humans.* Springer, 2016.

Bowers, C.A. *Education, Cultural Myths and the Ecological Crisis: Toward Deep Changes.* State University of New York Press, 1993.

Bracken, Harry M. *Descartes.* Oneworld Publications, 2002.

Buell, Frederick. *From Apocalypse to Way of Life.* Routledgc, 2003.

Buell, Lawrence. *Writing for an Endangered World Literature, Culture, And Environment in The U.S. and*

Beyond. The Belknap Press of Harvard University Press, 2001.

Bull, Malcolm, Anthony J. Cascardi and T.J. Clark. *Nietzsche's Negative Ecologies*. University of California Press, 2009.

Cain, P.J. and A.G. Hopkins. *British Imperialism: 1688-2015*. Routledge, 2016.

Calarco, Matthew. *Zoographies The Question of The Animal From Heidegger to Derrida*. Columbia University Press, 2008.

Callicott, J. Baird and Robert Frodeman eds. *Encyclopedia of Environmental Ethics and Philosophy*. Gale Cengage Learning, 2009.

Capra, Fritjof. *The Turning Point Science, Society and The Rising Culture*. Bantam Books, 1982.

Capra, Fritjof. *The Web of Life*. Anchor Books, 1996.

Carroll, Joseph. *Literary Darwinism Evolution, Human Nature and Literature*. Routledge, 2005.

Carson, Rachel. *Silent Spring*. Mariner Books, 2002.

Castree, Noel, Mike Hulme, and James D. Proctor eds. *Companion to Environmental Studies*. Routledge, 2018.

Cavanagh, Edward and Lorenzo Veracini eds. *The Routledge Handbook of The History of Settler Colonialism*. Routledge, 2017.

Ceballos, Gerard, Anne H. Ehrlich and Paul R. Ehrlich. *The Annihilation of Nature Human Extinction of Birds and Mammals*. Johns Hopkins University Press.

Chan, Jeffrey K.H. *Urban Ethics in the Anthropocene*. Palgrave Macmillan, 2019.

Christopolous, Menelaos, Efimia D. Karakantza and Olga Levaniouk eds. *Light and Darkness in Ancient Greek Myth and Religion*. Lexington Books, 2010.

Churchill, Ward. *Struggle for the Land Native North American Resistance to Genocide, Ecocide and Colonization*. City Lights, 2002.

Ciment, James ed. *Colonial America*. Sharpe Reference, 2013.

Clark, Timothy. *Ecocriticism on the Edge Anthropocentrism as a Threshold Concept*. Bloomsbury, 2015.

Clark, Timothy. *The Cambridge Introduction to Literature and the Environment*. Cambridge University Press, 2011.

Cook, Deborah. *Adorno on Nature*. Routledge, 2014.

Corrington, Robert S. *Deep Pantheism Toward a New Transcendentalism*. Lexington Books, 2016.

Corrington, Robert S. *Nature's Religion*. Rowman and Littlefield Publishers Inc., 1997.

Crist, Eileen and H. Bruce Rinker ed. *Gaia in Turmoil: Climate Change, Biodepletion, and Earth Ethics in an Age of Crisis*. The MIT Press, 2010.

Crosby, Donald A. *A Religion of Nature*. State University of New York Press, 2002.

Crutchfield, James A., Candy Moulton and Terry A Del Bene eds. *The Settlement of America*. Sharpe Reference, 2013.

Cruz, Laura and Willem Frijhoff eds. *Myth in History, History in Myth*. Brill, 2009.

Curtin, Jeremiah. *Creation Myths of Primitive America*. ABC CLIO, 2002.

Cusack, Carole M. *The Sacred Tree: Ancient and Medieval Manifestations*. Cambridge Scholars Publishing, 2011.

Danielou, Alain. *The Myths and Gods of India*. Simon & Schuster, 1991.

Dant, Sara. *Losing Eden An Environmental History of the American West*. Malden: Wiley Blackwell, 2017. Print.

Davies, Jeremy. *The Birth of the Anthropocene*. University of California Press, 2016.

De Chardin, Pierre Teilhard. *The Future of Man*. Norman Denny tr.Image Books, 2004.

De Chardin, Pierre Teilhard. *The Phenomenon of Man*. New York: Harper Perennial, 2008. Print.

De Jonge, Eccy. *Spinoza and Deep Ecology*. Routledge, 2016.

DeLoughrey, Elizabeth and George B. Handley. *Postcolonial Ecologies Literatures of the Environment*. Oxford University Press, 2011.

DeMello, Margo. *Animals and Society An Introduction to Human-Animal Studies*. Columbia University Press, 2012.

Desjardins, Joseph R. *Environmental Ethics An Introduction to Environmental Philosophy*. Wadsworth Cengage Learning, 2013.

Devall, Bill and George Sessions. *Deep Ecology*. Peregrine Smith Books, 1985.

Dhammika, S. *Nature and the Environment in Early Buddhism*. Buddha Dhamma Mandala Society, 2015.

Dowden, Ken and Niall Livingstone eds. *A Companion to Greek Mythology*. Wiley Blackwell, 2011.

Doyle, Timothy and Doug McEachern. *Environment and Politics*. Routledge, 2008. Print.

Drengson, Alan and Bill Deval eds. *The Ecology of Wisdom: Writings by Arne Naess*. Counterpoint, 2008.

Dunbar-Ortiz, Roxanne. *An Indigenous Peoples' History of the United States*. Beacon Press, 2014.

Eaton, Heather and Lois Ann Lorentzen eds. *Ecofeminism and Globalization*. Rowman and Littlefield

Publishers, Inc, 2003.

Eliade, Mircea. *Myth and Reality*. Willard R. Trask tr. Harper & Row Publishers, 1963.

Emmanuel, Steven M. ed. *A Companion to Buddhist Philosophy*. Wiley Blackwell, 2013.

Empson, Martin. *Land and Labour Marxism, Ecology and Human History*. Bookmarks Publication, 2014.

Erdoes, Richard and Alfonso Ortiz. *American Indian Myths and Legends*. Pantheon Books, 1984.

Falola, Toyin. *The Power of African Cultures*. University of Rochester Press, 2008.

Feder, Helena. *Ecocriticism and the Idea of Culture*. Ashgate, 2014.

Fee, Christopher and David Leeming. *The Goddess: Myths of the Great Mother*. Reaktion Books, 2016.

Fern, Richard L. *Nature, God and Humanity Envisioning an Ethics of Nature*. Cambridge University Press, 2004.

Flannery, Tim. *The Eternal Frontier An Ecological History of North America and Its People*. Grove Press, 2001.

Flood, Gavin ed. *The Blackwell Companion to Hinduism*. Blackwell Publishing, 2003.

Ford, Clyde W. *The Hero With an African Face: Mythic Wisdom of Traditional Africa*. Bantam Books, 1999.

Foster, John Bellamy, Brett Clark and Richard York. *The Ecological Rift: Capitalism's War on the Earth*. Monthly Review Press, 2010.

Foster, John Bellamy. *Marx's Ecology Materialism and Nature*. Monthly Review Press, 2000.

Franklin, Adrian. *Nature and Social Theory*. Sage Publications, 2002.

Fredriksen, John C. *Chronology of American History*. New York: New York: Facts on File, 2001. Print.

Fry, Stephen. *Mythos: The Greek Myths Retold*. Penguin, 2018.

Gaard, Greta ed. *Ecofeminism Women, Animals, Nature*. Temple University Press, 1993.

Garber, Daniel. *Descartes Embodied Reading Cartesian Philosophy Through Cartesian Science*. Cambridge University Press, 2009.

Gatta, John. *Making Nature Sacred: Literature, Religion, and Environment in America from the Puritans to the Present*. Oxford University Press, 2004.

Gersdorf, Catrin and Sylvia Mayer eds. *Nature in Literary and Cultural Studies*. Rodopi, 2006.

Gifford, Terry. *Pastoral The New Critical Idiom*. Routledge, 1999.

Gillam, Scott. *Rachel Carson Pioneer of Environmentalism*. Abdo Publishing, 2011.

Gomez, Michael A. *African Dominion: A New History of Empire in Early and Medieval West Africa*. Princeton University Press, 2018.

Goodenough, Ursula. *The Sacred Depths of Nature*. Oxford University Press, 1998.

Gottlieb, Roger S. ed. *The Oxford Handbook of Religion and Ecology*. Oxford University Press, 2006.

Gottlieb, Roger S. *This Sacred Earth: Religion, Nature, Environment*. Routledge, 2004.

Grant, Michael and John Hazel. *Who's Who in Classical Mythology*. Routledge, 2002.

Grant, Michael. *Myths of the Greeks and Romans*. Meridian, 1995.

Graves, Robert. *The Greek Myths*. Penguin Books, 2018.

Green, Miranda. *Animals in Celtic Life and Myth*. Routledge, 1998.

Griffin, John. *On the Origin of Beauty: Ecophilosophy in the Light of Traditional Wisdom*. World Wisdom, Inc., 2011.

Grusin, Richard ed. *Anthropocene Feminism*. University Press of Minnesota, 2017.

Gunn, Celia M. *Totem Animals*. Hampton Roads Publishing, Inc., 2016.

Guttman, Robert. *Eco-Capitalism*. Palgrave Macmillan, 2018.

Hahnel, Robin. *Green Economics Confronting the Ecological Crisis*. Routledge, 2011.

Hailwood, Simon. *Alienation and Nature in Environmental Philosophy*. Cambridge University Press, 2015.

Hamilton, Clive. *Defiant Earth: The Fate of Humans in the Anthropocene*. Allen & Unwin, 2017.

Hamilton, Edith. *Mythology*. Little, Brown and Company, 2017.

Hard, Robin. *The Routledge Handbook of Greek Mythology*. Routledge, 2004.

Hart, John ed. *The Wiley Blackwell Companion to Religion and Ecology*. Wiley Blackwell, 2017.

Heise, Ursula K. *Sense of Place and Sense of Planet*. Oxford University Press, 2008.

Hixson, Walter L. *American Settler Colonialism*. Palgrave Macmillan, 2013.

Horne, Gerald. *The Apocalypse of Settler Colonialism*. Monthly Review Press, 2017.

Huggan, Graham and Helen Tiffin. *Postcolonial Ecocriticism Literature, Animals, Environment*. New York: Routledge, 2010. Print.

Hughes, J. Donald. *An Environmental History of the World*. Routledge, 2001.

Humphrey, Mathew. *Preservation Versus the People*. Oxford University Press, 2002.

James, E.O. *The Cult of the Mother Goddess*. Thames and Hudson, 1959.

Jameson, Michael H. *Cults and Rites in Ancient Greece*. Cambridge University Press, 2014.

Jenkins, Willis. *Ecologies of Grace Environmental Ethics and Christian Theology*. Oxford University Press, 2008.

Johnston, Sarah Iles. *The Story of Myth*. Harvard University Press, 2018.

Jones, Constance A. and James D. Ryan. *Encyclopedia of Hinduism*. Facts on File, Inc., 2007.

Jones, Constance A. and James D. Ryan. *Encyclopedia of Hinduism*. New York: Facts on File, 2007. Print.

Katz, Eric, Andrew Light and David Rothenberg eds. *Beneath the Surface: Critical Essays in the Philosophy of Deep Ecology*. The MIT Press, 2000.

Kearns, Laurel and Catherine Keller eds. *Ecospirit: Religion, Philosophy and the Earth*. Fordham University Press, 2007.

Keown, Damien. *Buddhist Ethics A Very Short Introduction*. Oxford University Press, 2005.

Kinsley, David R. *Hindu Goddesses: Visions of the Divine Feminine in the Hindu Religious Tradition*. University of California Press, 1988.

Klein, Naomi. *This Changes Everything Capitalism vs Climate*. Simon & Schuster, 2015.

Knight, Richard L. and Suzanne Riedel eds. *Aldo Leopold and the Ecological Conscience*. Oxford University Press, 2002.

Knott, Kim. *Hinduism A Very Short Introduction.* Oxford University Press, 1998.

Krech, Shepard, J.R. McNeill and Carolyn Merchant eds. *Encyclopedia of World Environmental History Vol-1.* Routledge, 2004.

Krech, Shepard, J.R. McNeill and Carolyn Merchant eds. *Encyclopedia of World Environmental History Vol-2.* Routledge, 2004.

Krech, Shepard, J.R. McNeill and Carolyn Merchant eds. *Encyclopedia of World Environmental History Vol-3.* Routledge, 2004.

Krishna, Nanditha. *Hinduism and Nature.* Penguin Books, 2017.

Kroeber, Karl ed. *Native American Storytelling: A Reader of Myths and Legends.* Blackwell Publishing, 2007.

Larson, Jennifer. *Understanding Geek Religion.* Routledge, 2016.

Lear, Linda. *Rachel Carson Witness for Nature.* Boston: Mariner Books, 2009. Print.

Leeming, David A. *Creation Myths of the World.* ABC CLIO, 2010.

Leeming, David and Jake Page. *The Mythology of Native North America.* University of Oklahoma Press, 1998.

Leeming, David. *The World of Myths.* Oxford University Press, 1990.

LeMenager, Stephanie, Teresa Shewry and Ken Hiltner eds. *Environmental Criticism for Twenty-First Century.* Routledge, 2011.

Levin, Simon ed. *Encyclopedia of Biodiversity.* Academic Press, 2013.

Lewis, Jon E. *A Brief Guide to Native American Myths and Legends.* Constable and Robinson, 2013.

Lewis, Simon L. and Mark A. Maslin. *The Human Planet How We Created the Anthropocene.* Yale University Press, 2018.

Lochtfeld, James G. *The Illustrated Encyclopedia of Hinduism.* The Rosen Publishing Group, Inc, 2002.

Louise von Franz, Marie. *Creation Myths.* Shambhala, 2017.

Lupa. *Nature Spirituality from the Ground Up: Connect with Totems in Your Ecosystem.* Llewellyn Publications, 2016.

Lynch, Patricia Ann and Jeremy Roberts. *Native American Mythology A to Z.* Chelsea House Publishing, 2010.

Lynch, Patricia Ann. *African Mythology A to Z.* Chelsea House Publishers, 2010.

Mackenzie, Donald A. *Indian Myth and Legend.* Gresham Publishing Company, 1913.

MacLeod, Sharon Paice. *The Divine Feminine in Ancient Europe: Goddesses, Sacred Women and the Origins of Western Culture.* McFarland & Company, Inc., Publishers, 2014.

Marinatos, Nanno. *The Goddess and the Warrior.* Routledge, 2000.

Martin, Joel W. *Native American Religion.* Oxford University Press, 1999.

Matthews, Donald H. *Honoring the Ancestors: An African Cultural Interpretation of Black Religion and Literature.* Oxford University Press, 1998.

McClintock, James I. *Nature's Kindred Spirits.* The University of Wisconsin Press, 1994.

McDonald, Barry. *Seeing God Everywhere: Essays on Nature and the Sacred.* World Wisdom Inc., 2003.

McDonald, Hugh P. *Environmental Philosophy*. Rodopi, 2014.

McKibben, Bill. *The End of Nature: Humanity, Climate Change and the Natural World*. Bloomsbury, 2003.

McNeese, Tim. *Christopher Columbus and the Discovery of the Americas*. Chelsea House Publishers, 2006.

Merchant, Carolyn. *Ecology*. Humanity Books, 2008.

Merchant, Carolyn. *Radical Ecology The Search for a Livable World*. Routledge, 2005.

Merchant, Carolyn. *Reinventing Eden The Fate of Nature in Western Culture*. Routledge, 2003.

Merchant, Carolyn. *The Columbia Guide to American Environmental History*. Columbia University Press, 2002.

Merchant, Carolyn. *The Death of Nature Women, Ecology and the Scientific Revolution*. Harper and Row, Publishers, 1990.

Meredith, Martin. *The Fortunes of Africa: A 5000 Year History of Wealth, Greed and Endeavor*. Public Affairs, 2014.

Moore, Bryan L. *Ecology and Literature Ecocentric Personification from Antiquity to the Twenty First Century*. Palgrave Macmillan, 2008.

Moore, Jason W. *Capitalism in the Web of Life*. Verso, 2015.

Morales, Helen. *Classical Mythology: A Very Short Introduction*. Oxford University Press, 2007.

Morford, Mark P.O. and Robert J. Lenardon. *Classical Mythology*. Oxford University Press, 2003.

Moriarty, Michael. *Fallen Nature, Fallen Selves*. Oxford University Press, 2006.

Morton, Timothy. *Dark Ecology: For a Logic of Future Coexistence*. Columbia University Press, 2016.

Morton, Timothy. *Ecology Without Nature: Rethinking Environmental Aesthetics.* Harvard University Press, 2007.

Motz, Lotte. *The Faces of the Goddess.* Oxford University Press, 1997.

Naess, Arne. *Ecology, Community and Lifestyle.* David Rothenberg tr. Cambridge University Press, 1989.

Naess, Arne. *Ecology, Community and Lifestyle: Outline of an Ecosophy.* David Rothenberg tr. Cambridge University Press, 1989.

Nagle, Jeanne ed. *Native American Spirit Beings.* Britannica Educational Publishing, 2015.

Nelson, Lance E. *Purifying the Earthly Body of God: Religion and Ecology in Hindu India.* State University of New York Press, 1998.

Neumann, Erich. *The Great Mother: An Analysis of the Archetype.* Princeton University Press, 2015.

Newell, Peter. *Globalization and the Environment.* Polity Press, 2012.

Nichols, Larry A., George A. Mather and Alvin J. Schmidt eds. *Encyclopedic Dictionary of Cults, Sects and World Religions.* Zondervan, 2009.

Nicholsen, Shierry Weber. *The Love of Nature and the End of the World.* The MIT Press, 2002.

Northcott, Michael S. *Place, Ecology and the Sacred: The Moral Geography of Sustainable Communities.* Bloomsbury, 2015.

Nozedar, Adele. *The Element Encyclopedia of Native Americans.* Harper Element, 2013.

Ogden, Daniel ed. *A Companion to Greek Religion.* Blackwell Publishing, 2007.

Ohrem, Dominik and Roman Bartosch eds. *Beyond the Human Animal Divide Creaturely Lives in Literature and Culture*. Palgrave Macmillan, 2017.

Paper, Jordan. *Native North American Religious Traditions: Dancing for Life*. Praeger, 2007.

Parker, John and Richard Rathbone. *African History: A Very Short Introduction*. Oxford University Press, 2007.

Pepper, David. *Eco-Socialism: From Deep Ecology to Social Justice*. Routledge, 2003.

Philip, Neil. *Myths & Legends Explained*. Dorling Kindersley, 2007.

Phillips, Dana. *The Truth of Ecology Nature, Culture and Literature in America*. Oxford University Press, 2003.

Pinch, Geraldine. *Handbook of Egyptian Mythology*. ABC CLIO, 2002.

Pomeroy, Sarah B., Stanley M. Burstein, Walter Donlan et al. *A Brief History of Ancient Greece Politics, Society and Culture*. Oxford University Press, 2004.

Preece, Rod. *Animals and Nature: Cultural Myths, Cultural Realities*. UBC Press, 1999.

Purdy, Jedidah. *After Nature A Politics for the Anthropocene*. Harvard University Press, 2015.

Radice, William. *Myths and Legends of India Vol 1*. Penguin, 2016.

Raffnsoe, Sverre. *Philosophy of the Anthropocene*. Palgrave Macmillan, 2016.

Rappaport, Roy A. *Ecology, Meaning and Religion*. North Atlantic Books, 1979.

Rasmussen, Larry L. *Earth-Honoring Faith: Religious Ethics in a New Key*. Oxford University Press, 2013.

Remler, Pat. *Egyptian Mythology A to Z*. Chelsea House Publishing, 2010.

Rockwell, David. *Giving Voice to Bear: North American Indian Myths, Rituals and Images of the Bear*. Roberts Rinehart Publishers, 2003.

Rose, H.J. *A Handbook of Greek Mythology*. Routledge, 2005.

Rosen, Steven J. *Essential Hinduism*. Praeger, 2006.

Rue, Loyal. *Religion Is Not About God: How Spiritual Traditions Nurture Our Biological Nature And What to Expect When They Fail*. Rutgers University Press, 2005.

Ruether, Rosemary Radford. *Goddesses and the Divine Feminine*. University of California Press, 2005.

Sale, Kirkpatrick. *After Eden The Evolution of Human Domination*. Duke University Press, 2006.

Sax, Boria. *The Mythical Zoo: An Encyclopedia of Animals in World Myth, Legend & Literature*. ABC CLIO, 2001.

Scheid, Daniel P. *The Cosmic Common Good Religious Grounds for Ecological Ethics*. Oxford University Press, 2016.

Schliephake, Christopher ed. *Ecocriticism, Ecology and the Cultures of Antiquity*. Lexington Books, 2017.

Schwagerl, Christian. *The Anthropocene The Human Era and How it Shapes Our Planet*. Synergetic Press, 2014.

Segal, Robert A. *Myth: A Very Short Introduction*. Oxford University Press, 2004.

Selin, Helaine ed. *Nature Across Cultures: Views of Nature and Environment in Non-Western Cultures*. Springer, 2003

Sessions, George ed. *Deep Ecology for the Twenty First Century*. Shambhala, 1995.

Shaw, Ian. *Ancient Egypt: A Very Short Introduction*. Oxford University Press, 2004.

Shorrock, Robert. *The Myth of Paganism: Nonnus, Dionysius and the World of Late Antiquity*. Bloomsbury, 2011.

Singer, Peter. *Animal Liberation*. Ecco, 2002.

Sjoo, Monica and Barbara Mor. *The Great Cosmic Mother: Rediscovering the Religion of the Earth.* Harper San Francisco, 1991.

Smith, Tom. *Discovery of the Americas.* Facts on File, Inc., 2005.

Souder, William. *On a Farther Shore The Life and Legacy of Rachel Carson.* New York: Crown Publishers, 2012. Print.

Spence, Lewis. *Ancient Egyptian Myths and Legends.* Dover Publications, INC., 1990.

Sproul, Barbara C. *Primal Myths: Creation Myths from Around the World.* Harper One, 1979.

Starhawk. *The Earth Path: Grounding Your Spirit in the Rhythms of Nature.* Harper One, 2005.

Steiner, Gary. *Anthropocentrism and Its Discontents.* University of Pittsburgh Press, 2005.

Stoner, Alexander M. and Andony Melathopoulos. *Freedom in the Anthropocene: Twentieth Century Helplessness in the Face of Climate Change.* Palgrave Macmillan, 2015.

Strazzoni, Andrea. *Dutch Cartesianism and the Birth of Philosophy of Science.* De Gruyter, 2019.

Sullivan, Lawrence E. ed. *Native Religions and Cultures of North America: Anthropology of the Sacred.* Continuum, 2000.

Suzuki, David, Amanda McConnel and Adrienne Mason. *The Sacred Balance: Rediscovering Our Place in Nature.* Allen & Unwin, 2007.

Taylor, Nik. *Humans, Animals and Society An Introduction to Human-Animal Studies.* Lantern Books, 2013.

Taylor, Paul W. *Respect for Nature A Theory of Environmental Ethics.* Princeton University Press, 2011.

Tobias, Michael Charles and Jane Gray Morrison. *Anthrozoology Embracing Co-Existence in the Anthropocene.* Springer, 2017.

Townsend, Colin R., Michael Begon and John L. Harper. *Essentials of Ecology.* Blackwell Publishing, 2008.

Townsend, Kenneth W. *First Americans: A History of Native Peoples.* Routledge, 2019.

Varner, Gary E. *In Nature's Interests? Interests, Animal Rights, and Environmental Ethics.* Oxford University Press, 1998.

Varner, Gary R. *The Mythic Forest, The Green Man and The Spirit of Nature: The Re-Emergence of the Spirit of Nature from Ancient Times into Modern Society.* Algora Publishing, 2006.

Vaughan-Lee, Llewellyn ed. *Spiritual Ecology The Cry of the Earth.* The Golden Sufi Center, 2013.

Vetlesen, Johan Arne. *The Denial of Nature Environmental Philosophy in the Era of Global Capitalism.* Routledge, 2015.

Waldau, Paul and Kimberley Patton eds. *A Communion of Subjects: Animals in Religion, Science and Ethics.* Columbia University Press, 2006.

Wall, Derek. *Green History A Reader in Environmental Literature, Philosophy and Politics.* Routledge, 2004.

Warren, Karen J. *Ecofeminist Philosophy A Western Perspective on What It Is and Why It Matters.* Rowman and Littlefield Publishers, Inc, 2000.

Warren, Karen J. ed. *Ecofeminism Women, Culture, Nature.* Indiana University Press, 1997.

Washington, Haydn. *Healing the Planet Through Belonging.* Routledge, 2019.

Washington, Haydn. *Human Dependence on Nature.* Routledge, 2013.

Waterfield, Robin. *The Greek Myths: Stories of the Greek Gods and Heroes Vividly Retold.* Quercus, 2012.

Watson, Peter. *The Great Divide Nature and Human Nature in the Old World and the New.* Harper Perennial, 2013.

Weisman, Alan. *The World Without Us.* Thomas Dunne Books, 2007.

Wheeler, Stephen M. *Climate Change and Social Ecology.* Routledge, 2012.

Whitehead, Mark. *Environmental Transformations A Geography of the Anthropocene.* Routledge, 2014.

Williams, Chris. *Ecology and Socialism.* Haymarket Books, 2010.

Williams, George M. *Handbook of Hindu Mythology.* ABC CLIO, 2003.

Wirzba, Norman. *The Paradise of God: Renewing Religion in an Ecological Age.* Oxford University Press, 2003.

Witoszek, Nina and Andrew Brennan eds. *Philosophical Dialogues Arne Naess and the Progress of Ecophilosophy.* Rowman and Littlefield Publishers, Inc, 1999.

Witzel, E.J. Michael. *The Origins of the World's Mythologies.* Oxford University Press, 2012.

Woodard, Roger D. *The Cambridge Companion to Greek Mythology.* Cambridge University Press, 2007.

Worster, Donald. *The Wealth of Nature Environmental History and The Ecological Imagination.* Oxford University Press, 1993.

Worthy, Kenneth. *Invisible Nature Healing the Destructive Divide between People and the Environment.*

Prometheus Books, 2013.

Young, William A. *Quest for Harmony: Native American Spiritual Traditions*. Seven Bridges Press, 2001.

Zimmer, Heinrich. *Myths and Symbols in Indian Art and Civilization*. Joseph Campbell ed. Pantheon Books, 1946.

9 798885 309332

Printed by Libri Plureos GmbH in Hamburg, Germany